THE TEMPERAMENT
MODEL OF BEHAVIOR

Understanding Your Natural Tendencies

For you
Gracie
[signature]

JOHN T. COCORIS, PSY. D.

6/2018

The Temperament Model of Behavior
©2014 By Dr. John T. Cocoris

All rights reserved. No part of this book may be reproduced in any form, except for the inclusion of brief quotations in a review, without permission in writing from the author:

John T. Cocoris
7209 Verdi Way
McKinney, TX 75070
(972) 529-9150

johncocoris@sbcglobal.net
www.fourtemperaments.com

ISBN 0-9721650-1-0
Library of Congress Card Number:

Profile Dynamics
McKinney, Texas 75070

Cover and interior design by April Beltran

Acknowledgments

I am indebted to my close friend and associate Leroy Hamm who has shared my vision and my passion for over a quarter of a century. We have spent countless hours talking about observations we have both made concerning people and temperaments. He has read and reread the manuscript, making helpful suggestions. I would also like to thank the following people for their helpful suggestions and for editing this work: Darrellene Cocoris, Mike Cocoris, Gary Fusco, Lane Hedgepeth, Mercedes Hamm and Joyce Jones. A special thanks to April Beltran who read and edited the manuscript offering insightful suggestions that has made this work better. April is also responsible for the interior layout and the book cover design.

CONTENTS

Contents

INTRODUCTION
IT BEGINS WITH "WHY?"

Have you ever wondered, "Why are people different?" Or "Why do I do what I do?" The Greek philosopher Theophrastus (d. 287 BC) was also curious. When he was in his 90's he wrote *Characters*, a book on personality. He raised a question that has encouraged the study of personality and individual differences ever since: "Why is it that while all Greece lies under the same sky and all the Greeks are educated alike, nevertheless we are all different with respect to personality?"

Hans J. Eysenck, in *Personality and Individual Differences, A Natural Science Approach*, 1985, quotes Roback (1931): "It is thanks to these writers of antiquity and their imitators that we can say with a high degree of confidence that human nature, though ages and oceans apart, is about the same wherever found, i.e., the same differences among individuals will be discovered whether they be ancient Greeks or 20th Century Americans."

People are different primarily because they possess different natural traits or tendencies, referred to as temperament. There are other factors that make us different including gender, when we were born, the culture in which we were raised, education, and how we responded to these experiences. Nothing, however, influences daily behavior like your natural tendencies or temperament.

Temperament refers to a person's natural disposition, the way in which one will consistently behave. The temperament model of behavior recognizes that people are born with natural ways of behaving, such as being assertive, sociable, passive, or analytical.

The oldest labels assigned to each of the four temperaments dates back to Galen (AD 129-200 or 216): Choleric, Sanguine, Phlegmatic, and Melancholy. The most popular terms used today were coined by Dr. John Geier in the early

1970's: High D (Choleric), High I (Sanguine), High S (Phlegmatic) and High C (Melancholy). Because these terms are widely recognized they are included throughout this work.

Each of the four primary temperaments will have a different behavioral style as illustrated below:

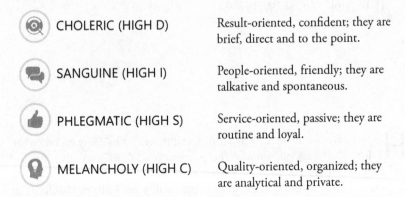

CHOLERIC (HIGH D) — Result-oriented, confident; they are brief, direct and to the point.

SANGUINE (HIGH I) — People-oriented, friendly; they are talkative and spontaneous.

PHLEGMATIC (HIGH S) — Service-oriented, passive; they are routine and loyal.

MELANCHOLY (HIGH C) — Quality-oriented, organized; they are analytical and private.

PART I

BACKGROUND & FOUNDATIONAL PRINCIPLES

NOTE:

Understanding the origins and the foundational principles behind temperaments are imperative in understanding your and other's temperaments. Chapters one through five will serve as the foundation to build upon when we discuss the temperament and temperament blends. Without this foundation, the temperament model of behavior can be misused and misinterpreted, therefore diluting its ability to support you and others.

CHAPTER **ONE**

HISTORY AND DEVELOPMENT OF
THE TEMPERAMENT CONCEPT

Throughout history there have been many attempts to explain why people are different. One of the first systems developed was astrology, which looked outside of man to explain the differences. The astrological system is made up of twelve signs.

The idea that a person's behavior is the result of being born with natural traits or tendencies (temperament) has been around for at least 2,400 years. The men and women listed below are the pioneers that have made the most significant contributions to the development of this concept.

HIPPOCRATES (C. 460-377 B.C.)

Hippocrates is given credit for observing that people have natural tendencies (temperament). He looked inside of man to explain the differences in people's behavior. He taught that behavior was determined by the presence of an excessive amount of one of four fluids or humors: yellow bile (Chlor), red bile or blood (Sangis), white bile (Phlegm) or black bile (Melan).

These four humors were thought to be related to the four elements of earth, air, fire, and water. Hippocrates and other early Greeks believed that an excess of one of the four humors produced a particular temperament and behavior.

According to Hippocrates, the four bodily fluids also influenced a person's health. He postulated that an imbalance among the humors (blood, phlegm, black bile, and yellow bile) resulted in pain and disease and that good health was achieved through a balance of the four humors. He suggested that glands had a controlling effect on this balance. For many centuries this idea was held as the foundation of medicine. Since the time of Hippocrates the temperament concept was used as the basic explanation for why people do what they do. The temperament concept began to lose popularity, however, when modern psychology began in 1879.

The word temperament comes from the Latin word *temperamentum* and means "right blending." Hippocrates thought that a person's temperament was made up of a blending of the four humors.

YELLOW BILE | An excess of yellow bile resulted in a temperament (later called Choleric) believed to be warm/hot and dry and associated with the element of fire. The Choleric is result-oriented and tends to be quick to anger and action. This person is confident, decisive, domineering, independent, and productive. The Choleric likes to be in control.

RED BILE | An excess of red bile resulted in a temperament (later called Sanguine) believed to be warm/hot and wet and associated with the element of air. The Sanguine is people-oriented and tends to be carefree and full of hope. This person is sociable, enthusiastic, undisciplined, talkative, carefree, and has many friends. The Sanguine likes to have fun.

WHITE BILE | An excess of white bile resulted in a temperament (later called Phlegmatic) believed to be cool/cold and wet and associated with the element of water. The Phlegmatic is service-oriented and tends to be slow to motion and showing emotion. This person is calm, dependable, easygoing, and indecisive. The Phlegmatic likes a routine.

BLACK BILE | An excess of black bile resulted in a temperament (later called Melancholy) believed to be cool/cold and dry and associated with the element of earth. The Melancholy is quality-oriented and tends to take most everything seriously, especially their work. This person tends to be a perfectionist and is thoughtful, serious, worried, suspicious, rigid, and sensitive to criticism. The Melancholy likes to have a plan.

Hippocrates and the early Greeks were accurate in their observations of behavior but were incorrect about the origin of these tendencies. They are not, of course, created by the excess of a fluid. Today, we would say that they originate from some genetic predisposition, although we cannot be certain.

GALEN (AD 129-200 OR 216)

Galen was a Greek physician who lived 600 years after Hippocrates and was responsible for popularizing the temperaments during his time and relating them to illness. He is also credited with coining the terms Choleric, Sanguine, Phlegmatic, and Melancholy in his dissertation, *De temperamentis.*

NICHOLAS CULPEPER (1616-1654)

Nicholas Culpeper was an English botanist, herbalist, physician, and astrologer. He was the first to dispute two fundamental concepts that had existed since the time of Hippocrates. First, he rejected the idea that the four humors were the cause of a person's temperament. Second, he was the first to say that a person is influenced by two temperaments, one primary and one secondary. Before Culpeper, it was believed that a person was influenced by only one temperament.

IMMANUEL KANT (1724-1804)

Immanuel Kant, a German philosopher, described the temperaments in his book, *Anthropology from a Pragmatic Point of View*, 1798. The following excerpts show the consistency and enduring nature of human behavior:

> The Choleric Temperament of the Hot-Blooded Man. We say of a choleric man that he is fiery, burns up quickly like straw-fire, and can be readily appeased if others give in to him; there is no hatred in his anger, and in fact he loves someone all the more for promptly giving in to him.

> The Sanguine Temperament of The Volatile Man. A Sanguine person is carefree and attaches great importance to each thing for the moment, and the next moment may not give it another thought. He is a good companion, high-spirited, and all men are his friends.

> The Phlegmatic Temperament of the Cold-Blooded Man. Phlegma means apathy, dullness; phlegma as weakness is a tendency to inactivity, not to let oneself be moved even by strong incentives for getting busy. He is not easily angered, but reflects first whether he should get angry.

The Melancholy Temperament of the Grave Man. A man disposed to melancholy attaches great importance to everything that has to do with himself. He finds grounds for apprehension everywhere and directs his attention first to the difficulties. The melancholy temperament thinks deeply.

WILLIAM M. MARSTON (1893-1947)

William M. Marston was the first to contribute scientific evidence that people fit into one of four categories. He published his book, *Emotions of Normal People* in 1928 using the terms Dominant, Influence, Steadiness and Compliance.

Marston studied the emotions of normal people and through his observations identified four distinctively different behavioral styles. He then identified 35 words or phrases that characterized these four behavioral styles according to their emotional response in a favorable and unfavorable situation.

According to Dr. Marston's research, each behavioral style (or temperament) has a different response when faced with either a favorable or unfavorable environment. First, there is a neurological event caused by the perception of the stimuli in the environment (favorable or unfavorable). Second, a message is sent to the motor self (that which causes motion) to either move toward the stimuli, to move away from the stimuli, or not to move at all. Here are the four categories and the summary of his findings:

DOMINANCE [Choleric] | This person has active, positive movement in an unfavorable (antagonistic) environment to overcome the opposition.

INFLUENCE [Sanguine] | This person has active, positive movement in an favorable or friendly environment to enjoy socializing.

STEADINESS [Phlegmatic] | This person is passive in both a favorable and unfavorable environment.

COMPLIANCE [Melancholy] | This person has two responses in an unfavorable (antagonistic) environment. The first response is to withdraw. After the situation has been analyzed, and a plan developed, the second response is to be assertive in order to bring resolve. In a favorable environment they will move forward to enforce the rules and offer organization.

OLE HALLESBY (1879-1961)

Ole Hallesby, a Lutheran theology professor in Norway, contributed penetrating insight into the behavior of the temperaments. In his book, *Temperament And The Christian Faith*, written in the 1930's, he used the terms Choleric, Sanguine, Phlegmatic, and Melancholy. Hallesby's work is limited in that he discussed behavior as it related to the four primary temperaments and did not write about the dynamics of the blends. However, his insights into the behavior of the temperaments are unsurpassed in the writings that I have reviewed. For the serious student of the temperaments, this book is a must.

TIM LAHAYE (1926-   )

Tim LaHaye was the first to popularize the temperament concept within the Christian community. Dr. LaHaye published the first of several books in the 1960's using the terms Choleric, Sanguine, Phlegmatic, and Melancholy. He was the first to write in detail about the dynamics of the temperament blends.

JOHN G. GEIER (1934-2009)

John G. Geier built on the previous works of William M. Marston (1928), Walter Clarke (1940) and John Cleaver (1950). Walter Clarke developed the Activity Vector Analysis using the four dimensions of Aggressive, Sociable, Stable and Avoidant. Building on Clarke's work, John Cleaver created a 24-question, forced-choice instrument. From those, John Geier developed the Personal Profile instrument in 1972 (later called the Personal Profile System, 1977) that identified an individual's behavioral style (temperament blend). John Geier coined the terms High D (Dominant), High I (Influencing), High S (Steadiness), and High C (Competent).

OTHERS

Others have contributed to the temperament model of behavior using different terms, including Plato (350 BC), Paracelsus (1530), Adickes (1905), Spranger (1914), Kretschmer (1930), Adler (1937), Fromm (1947), Keirsey (1970), and Eysenck (1951).

TEMPERAMENT MODEL DEVIATIONS

The researchers mentioned above have maintained the original concept of the four temperaments and have expanded our knowledge with their insights. There have been others, however, who have deviated from the historical flow of the original four temperaments by renaming them and adding concepts that have caused confusion rather than clarity. Included in these, in my opinion, are Carl Jung and Isabel Myers. Both have been criticized for their lack of clarity and contradictions.

CARL JUNG (1875-1961)

Carl Jung, a Swiss psychiatrist, published *Psychological Types* in 1921. He was searching for answers as to why people were different. The premise of his work was to determine how people take in information and make decisions.

Jung coined the terms extrovert and introvert, suggesting that everyone falls into one of the two categories. The extrovert prefers the outer, objective world of things, people and actions; and the introvert prefers the inner, subjective world of thoughts, ideas, and emotions.

Jung identified four mental functions that he combined with extroversion and introversion: thinking (logical, objective); feeling (subjective experience); sensation (stimuli from the senses); and intuitive (creative, imaginative and integrative). Jung's system has eight basic personality types: extroverted thinker, extroverted feeler, extroverted sensor, extroverted intuitor, introverted thinker, introverted feeler, introverted sensor, and introverted intuitor.

There is some correlation between Jung's system and the original four temperaments by Hippocrates, but at best it is not clear. Jung made a valuable contribution by giving us the concepts of extrovert and introvert.

ISABEL MYERS (1897-1980) AND KATHARINE BRIGGS (1875-1968)

Isabel Myers and her mother, Katheryn Briggs, wrote a paper in 1958 titled, "Myers-Briggs Type Indicator (MBTI)" in which they proposed that there are sixteen different personality types. Their work was based on Carl Jung's writings on psychological types. In their system, a person has two choices for orientation; introvert (I) or extrovert (E); two choices for method of information intake sensing (S) or intuition (N); two choices for method of judgment, thinking (T) or feeling (F); and two choices to use in the outer world judgment (J) or perception (P). These combine to make up 16 personality types.

The Myers-Briggs Type Indicator is a popular and widely used instrument, but it is not without controversy. David J. Pittenger, Ph.D. made the following comments in his evaluation of the MBTI: "There are several reports of the test retest reliabilities of the four dimensions of the MBTI (Carskadon, 1977, 1979b; Howes & Carskadon, 1979; Stricker & Ross, 1962). These reports offer a consistent pattern that suggests that the reliability of the MBTI does not meet expectations derived from its theory" (Cautionary Comments Regarding the Myers-Briggs Type Indicator, published in 2005 in Consulting Psychology Journal: Practice and Research, Vol. 57, No. 3, 214).

SUMMARY

The ancient Greeks observed people and speculated on the reasons for their behavior. Their observations were supported in later centuries by a wide variety of people including medical doctors and philosophers. In the early 1900's, the scientific method was applied by Marston with the same results. The concept that people fall into four categories has been observed for over two thousand years, verified by the scientific method, and everyone describes them basically the same. The four temperaments illustrate the consistency and enduring nature of human behavior.

In *Personality and Individual Differences, A Natural Science Approach,* 1985 (p. 3), Hans J. Eysenck (1916-1997) sums up the concept of the four temperaments this way:

> This was pioneered by Hippocrates and later canonized by Galen, a Roman physician who lived in the second century A.D. It is to these men and to the many others who worked in this field that we owe the doctrine of the four temperaments: phlegmatic, sanguine, choleric, and melancholy. The highly successful typology thus established all those years ago was based on careful observation and provided a paradigm for scientific investigation that has lasted over 2,000 years and may still have something to teach us.

CHAPTER **TWO**

OVERVIEW OF THE PRIMARY TEMPERAMENTS

There are four primary temperaments. Two temperaments are extroverts, Choleric (High D) and Sanguine (High I), and two are introverts, Phlegmatic (High S) and Melancholy (High C). Extroverts are active and process oriented. From their point of view, the environment is made to provide the satisfaction that they want. Introverts tend to be passive, private, and accommodating. They tend to adapt to whatever the environment has to offer. They are production oriented.

The four temperaments combine to produce twelve blends. These twelve blends are expressed in fifteen patterns. More explanation will be given in chapters 6 through 9. The following is a brief explanation of the four primary temperaments.

 CHOLERIC | The Choleric is extroverted, hot-tempered, quick thinking, active, practical, strong-willed, easily annoyed, and result-oriented. The Choleric has a huge ego, a firm expression, and is self-confident, self-sufficient, and very independent minded. They are decisive, opinionated and find it easy to make decisions for themselves as well as others.

 SANGUINE | The Sanguine is extroverted, impulsive, fun-loving, activity-prone, entertaining, persuasive, easily amused, optimistic, and people-oriented. The Sanguine tends to be competitive, impulsive, and disorganized. The voice of the Sanguine will show excitement and friendliness. They have a natural smile and talk easily and often. They are animated, excitable, and accepting of others. They build relationships quickly and have lots of friends.

 PHLEGMATIC | The Phlegmatic is introverted, calm, unemotional, slow moving, easygoing, accommodating, and service-oriented. The Phlegmatic does not show much emotion and will have a stoic expression. They are slow to warm up and indirect when interacting with others. The Phlegmatic lives a quiet, peaceful, routine life, free of the normal anxieties of the other temperaments. They avoid getting too involved with people and life.

 MELANCHOLY | The Melancholy is introverted, logical, analytical, factual, private, conscientious, timid, and quality-oriented. The Melancholy will (most always) have a serious expression. They usually respond to others in a slow, cautious, and indirect manner. They are self-sacrificing, creative, and can be perfectionists. The Melancholy has high standards to avoid mistakes.

NOTE | Because a person's temperament represents such dominant needs, no one can hide or deny their temperament for very long. A person's behavior will usually represent their primary temperament 70% of the time.

DESCRIPTIVE WORDS

The descriptive words listed below (Figure 1) represent the essence of what it means to be that particular temperament. For example, the group of 28 words listed under Choleric (High D) are characteristic of a person who has the Choleric temperament. The intensity of expression of any trait will vary from person to person.

FIGURE 1

PRIMARY TEMPERAMENT DESCRIPTIONS

CHOLERIC HIGH D	SANGUINE HIGH I	PHLEGMATIC HIGH S	MELANCHOLY HIGH C
Direct	Impulsive	Patient	Conscientious
Daring	Influential	Passive	Cautious
Decisive	Impressionable	Predictable	Competent
Demanding	Enthusiastic	Possessive	Compliant
Domineering	Emotional	Procrastinates	Critical
Determined	Energetic	Tolerant	Systematic/accurate
Doer	Entertaining	Loyal	Needs facts, logic
Confident	Optimistic	Needs routine	Needs time to think
Likes to achieve	Articulate	Dependent	Needs plan/privacy
Wants results	Lacks follow-through	Supportive	Anticipates problems
Visionary	Charming	Deliberate	Likes quality
Goal-oriented	Needs to talk	Harmonious	Inquisitive
Easily bored	Likes to play	Closed	Indecisive
Easily annoyed	Likes to win	Team-player	Perfectionist
Takes action	Sociable	Accommodating	Pessimistic
Likes pressure	Approachable	Holds grudges	Guilt feelings
Needs a challenge	Unorganized	Quiet	Diplomatic
Problem-solver	Generous	Indecisive	Restrained
Risk-taker	Poised	Stable	Analytical
Independent	Persuasive	Resists change	Avoids conflict
Self-reliant	Personable	Agreeable	Likes details
Energetic	Trusting	Complacent	Evasive

TEMPERAMENT DOMINANCE & BEHAVIOR

Each person possesses all four temperaments. One temperament will be the most dominant and one will be the least dominant with the other two somewhere in-between. Noted below are the differences in behavior when a particular temperament is either most or least.

CHOLERIC | HIGH D

MOST

When the Choleric (D) is the first temperament, the individual will take an active, assertive, direct approach to obtaining results. They can easily overwhelm others with their assertiveness.

LEAST

When the Choleric is the least temperament, the individual will obtain results in a more organized, deliberate, and calculated manner. They will have significant difficulty confronting others, being assertive, and stating an opinion.

SANGUINE | HIGH I

MOST

When the Sanguine is the first temperament, the individual will approach new people in an outgoing, gregarious, and socially assertive manner. They tend to be impulsive, emotional, reactive, and will seek attention, affection, and touch.

LEAST

When the Sanguine is the least temperament, the individual will approach new people in a more congenial, controlled, sincere, and reserved manner. They tend to place importance on the control of emotions, being sincere, and taking a mostly logical approach to people and events.

PHLEGMATIC | HIGH S

MOST

When the Phlegmatic is the first temperament, the individual will prefer a more controlled, deliberate, and predictable environment. They value security of the situation, discipline, and routine behavior. This person needs time to adjust to change and help in making decisions.

LEAST

When the Phlegmatic is the least temperament, the individual prefers a more flexible, dynamic, and unstructured environment.

MELANCHOLY | HIGH C

MOST

When the Melancholy is the first temperament, this individual prefers that things are done the right way, according to established or accepted standards.

LEAST

When the Melancholy is the least temperament, this individual will operate more independently. Their theme is, "the right way is my way or no way."

TENDENCY RATINGS

Each temperament is more naturally able to express certain behaviors or tendencies than another. Understanding the natural tendencies that a person possess will help align expectations of what that person is capable of doing. Keep in mind that modification is possible during the maturing process. For example, one may have a tendency to resist change, but they may choose to be more flexible. Below are the tendency ratings of each temperament from the highest natural tendency for that behavior to the lowest tendency for that behavior.

ACTIVE

AFFECTIONATE

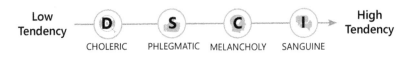

ASSERTIVE

FLEXIBILITY

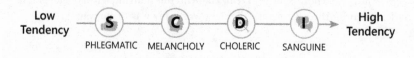

CONSISTENCY

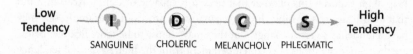

WILLINGNESS TO LISTEN

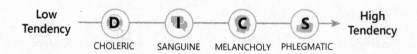

LOGICAL

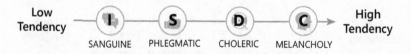

PATIENT

Low Tendency — **D** CHOLERIC — **I** SANGUINE — **C** MELANCHOLY — **S** PHLEGMATIC → High Tendency

SELF-DISCIPLINED

Low Tendency — **I** SANGUINE — **S** PHLEGMATIC — **D** CHOLERIC — **C** MELANCHOLY → High Tendency

SPONTANEOUS

Low Tendency — **S** PHLEGMATIC — **C** MELANCHOLY — **D** CHOLERIC — **I** SANGUINE → High Tendency

TRUSTING

Low Tendency — **D** CHOLERIC — **C** MELANCHOLY — **S** PHLEGMATIC — **I** SANGUINE → High Tendency

VERBAL SKILLS

Low Tendency — **S** PHLEGMATIC — **C** MELANCHOLY — **D** CHOLERIC — **I** SANGUINE → High Tendency

RESULT-ORIENTED

PEOPLE-ORIENTED

SERVICE-ORIENTED

QUALITY-ORIENTED

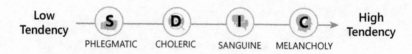

NOTE | There is a way of behaving which you feel is right, good, and normal.
This represents your "temperament comfort zone" of behavior.

PRIMARY TEMPERAMENT SUMMARY

The Four Primary Temperament chart (Figure 2) summarizes the differences between the primary temperaments. The chart has two axes: Extrovert/Introvert and Task/People to show which temperament is more naturally inclined to each.

The chart also shows each primary temperament's natural orientations, their basic traits, the estimated percentage of that particular temperament in the general population, the basic questions each temperament will likely need answered and their overall outlook in life.

PRIMARY TEMPERAMENT SUMMARY CHART
FIGURE 2

EXTROVERTS

CHOLERIC | DOMINANCE

Result-Oriented
Driver
Confident   10%
Brief   of population
Direct
To the point

Asks: "What?"

Positive Outlook

SANGUINE | INFLUENCE

People-Oriented
Expressive
35%   Friendly
of population   Talkative
Impulsive
Playful

Asks: "Who?

Positive Outlook

TASK
PEOPLE

PEOPLE
TASK

PHLEGMATIC | STEADINESS

Service-Oriented
Amiable
Routine
Loyal
Non-emotional
Non-assertive

Asks: "How?"   25%
of population

Neutral Outlook

MELANCHOLY | COMPLIANCE

Quality-Oriented
Analytical
Cautious
Private
Detailed
Independent

30%   Asks: "Why?"
of population

Negative Outlook

INTROVERTS

PRIMARY TEMPERAMENT SUMMARY

PRIMARY TEMPERAMENT SUMMARY CHART

CHAPTER **THREE**

NINE FUNDAMENTAL CONCEPTS

The temperament model of behavior is based on nine fundamental concepts. Understanding these concepts is essential to correctly applying the temperament model to behavior.

ONE | EVERYONE HAS TRAITS OF ALL FOUR TEMPERAMENTS

No one is totally deficient in any one of the temperaments. This allows an individual to demonstrate the traits of any of the four temperaments when the need arises. It is sufficient to know your primary and secondary temperaments, which create the greatest influence on behavior. There are, however, important influences coming from the alignment of the third and fourth temperaments. It is beyond the scope of this work to investigate the impact of such alignments.

TWO | TYPICAL BEHAVIOR IS THE BLEND OF TWO TEMPERAMENTS

Everyone has traits of all four temperaments but not all four are present with equal influence. The primary temperament will have a stronger influence on behavior than the other three. Of the remaining three, the secondary temperament will have a stronger influence on behavior than the remaining two. The second temperament will always modify the tendencies of the primary temperament in some significant way. The blend of the primary and secondary temperaments will represent a person's normal, usual and daily demeanor.

A pure temperament does not exist, i.e., no one is just one temperament. For example, there are three blends of the Choleric temperament: Choleric-Sanguine, Choleric-Phlegmatic, and Choleric-Melancholy. This is also true of the other three temperaments, making a total of twelve combinations.

A person's primary temperament undergoes significant change due to the influence of the secondary temperament. All three blends of a particular temperament will be similar in many ways but will also be different in many ways. For example, consider the Sanguine temperament: The Sanguine-Choleric really likes being with people or being active all the time. The Sanguine-Phlegmatic likes being around people most of the time, but some of the time they like to be alone to rest. The Sanguine-Melancholy likes to be around people most of the time, but some of the time they like to be alone to process information and plan. The three are similar in many ways but also quite different due to the influence of the secondary temperament.

One popular author, Florence Littauer (1992), has stated in her book, *Personality Plus*, that the Sanguine-Melancholy and the Choleric-Phlegmatic are unnatural combinations and therefore, do not exist. She claims that these are the result of personality masking and are not natural birth personality combinations because they are diametrically opposite. The conclusion was drawn based on faulty reasoning without research or personal interviews. This inaccuracy shows a lack of understanding of the temperament model. Has she never heard of a bi-polar person? Tim LaHaye, who has written numerous books on this subject, includes the Sanguine-Melancholy and Choleric-Phlegmatic blends when discussing the twelve combinations of the four temperaments. These blends, as well as the others (total of 12) are verifiable when research is founded upon interviewing people.

NOTE | A major benefit of knowing your temperament blend is that it will increase your self-awareness. According to Johari's Window, we all have blind spots—things that others see but we do not (see the Appendix).
You will become more aware of your natural strengths and natural weaknesses. Once aware, you will be able to consciously use your strengths and consciously work on overcoming your weaknesses. You will be able to identify specific needs that, when met, will enable you to live a more fulfilling life. Knowing about the temperaments will also help you see why people are different which will increasing your appreciation for a

different approach. Everyone has a natural, normal way of approaching people and events based on their temperament blend.

THREE | EACH TEMPERAMENT HAS NATURAL STRENGTHS AND WEAKNESSES

Each person will naturally excel at certain tasks while being naturally deficient in performing other tasks. For example, the Sanguine works well with people but is usually weak when working with details, whereas the Melancholy works well with details but will shy away from too much involvement with people.

FOUR | STRENGTHS AND WEAKNESSES REPRESENT BOTH TEMPERAMENTS

All twelve blends will combine strengths and weaknesses representing both temperaments. For example, the Choleric-Melancholy will combine the strengths and weakness of both the Choleric and the Melancholy. This produces a person who gets results with a detailed plan and can be forceful, explosive, and critical, but can also be gentle and sensitive.

FIVE | STRENGTHS AND WEAKNESSES VARY IN DEGREES OF INTENSITY

The intensity of traits present has significant influence on the expression of a person's temperament tendencies. Therefore, two people with the same temperament blend may demonstrate differences in behavior since there are at least three levels of expression of all the temperament blends:

CLASSIC

The tendencies of both temperaments are obvious and dominate a person's demeanor.

MODERATE

The tendencies of both temperaments are less intense and less dramatic in a person's demeanor.

MILD

The tendencies of both temperaments are less obvious in a person's demeanor.

Let's use the Sanguine-Phlegmatic blend to illustrate the idea. In some (classic), the Sanguine-Phlegmatic is so intense that they are almost overwhelming in their initial greeting—lots of smiles, touching, and openness. In others (moderate), the Sanguine-Phlegmatic blend is not as intense, and they are a bit reserved in their greeting, less smiling and slower to warm up. Still others (mild) are very slow to warm up, slow to smile, and present a laid-back demeanor.

A good friend of mine whom I've known since 1970 has the Sanguine-Phlegmatic blend. He was a successful business owner with about six hundred employees in his company throughout the state of Tennessee. On a visit to his home office, he introduced me and my wife to many of his staff. He could not walk past one employee without hugging them and saying something indicating that he knew them personally. Everyone loved their boss! He is a classic expression of the Sanguine-Phlegmatic temperament blend.

Another friend of mine has the same Sanguine-Phlegmatic temperament blend and he is a very successful salesperson. He does not demonstrate much emotion like the business owner. He is more subtle and laid-back. At first, it was difficult to determine his blend because he did not greet people with a smile. It took him a short time to warm up before you could see the Sanguine-Phlegmatic tendencies clearly. He is a mild expression of the Sanguine-Phlegmatic temperament blend.

The intensity principle is very important when identifying a person's temperament blend. Remember, people with the exact same temperament blend may present very different expressions because of the intensity difference that is inherent and unique to that particular person.

Some writers have presented the Sanguine temperament as one who always acts a certain way: a talkative, bounce-off-the-wall person, like Lucille Ball, who always loved being in front of a crowd. This characterization is simply not accurate. Many with the Sanguine temperament would go into cardiac arrest at the thought of getting up in front of a group. What prevents them from speaking to a group is, perhaps, a fear of rejection or the fear of being embarrassed if they make a mistake.

It is a serious misrepresentation to say that all people with a particular temperament blend act a certain way. This is worth repeating. People with the exact same temperament blend may present very different expressions because of the intensity difference that is inherent and unique to that person.

Sometimes you will see a very strong, intense, even overwhelming expression of a particular temperament blend. The following is an illustration of one who was probably Sanguine-Choleric: I was in a bank some years ago waiting at a teller's window to make a transaction. A few feet away a man was being very loud talking to another teller. I looked over to see him leaning over the counter into her face saying loudly, "smile honey, smile, it won't hurt you to smile honey, smile!" The teller had that deer-in-the-headlight look on her face. This man embarrassed her (and himself) with such an intense expression of his Sanguine temperament.

NOTE | People with the exact same temperament blend may present very different expressions because of the intensity difference that is inherent and unique to that person.

SIX | A STRENGTH OVEREXTENDED BECOMES A WEAKNESS

Any strength that is overextended (used to an extreme) will turn into a weakness. For example, the Choleric is naturally brief, direct, and to the point in their communication with others, but if they are too direct they become blunt and offensive. The Sanguine tends to talk a lot, but if they talk too much they will annoy others. The Phlegmatic is naturally accommodating, but if they are too accommodating others will take advantage of them. The Melancholy is naturally analytical, but if they are too analytical they will be paralyzed and never get anything done. Too much of a good thing is not always a good thing.

SEVEN | STRENGTHS CAN BE DEVELOPED AND WEAKNESSES CAN BE OVERCOME

Each person has the choice to develop their natural temperament strengths and overcome their natural temperament weaknesses. Whether or not a strength is developed or a weakness is overcome, and to what degree, depends on the individual's motivation. For example, the Choleric has a natural tendency to dominate people and events, but they may choose to not demonstrate this tendency in all situations because he or she has learned that it is not appropriate and such behavior harms relationships. The Sanguine has a tendency to be impulsive, but may choose not to demonstrate this tendency because he or she has learned that it has, at times, caused them difficulty. The Phlegmatic has a tendency to procrastinate, but may choose not to demonstrate this tendency because he or she has learned that it is not productive. The Melancholy has a tendency to be picky, but may choose not to demonstrate this tendency because he or she has learned that, at times, it frustrates others.

IT'S A CHOICE TO USE YOUR NATURAL STRENGTHS

Each individual develops the traits of his temperament to different levels. For example, two people with the same degree of the Melancholy temperament may express it very differently. One may be very organized and the other only somewhat organized. Both have the same tendency to organize; however, one may decide to develop the tendency more than the other.

IT'S A CHOICE TO OVERCOME YOUR NATURAL WEAKNESSES

Even though a particular weakness is natural to a temperament blend, it does not mean that an individual will always demonstrate that weakness in their behavior. It is possible to learn how to control and overcome the natural weaknesses associated with a temperament blend. It is a choice.

EIGHT | TEMPERAMENT TENDENCIES ARE DEVELOPED ACCORDING TO A PERSON'S RESPONSE TO THE VARIABLES IN THEIR ENVIRONMENT

Differences in behavior may also be explained by an individual's response to the many variables to which a person is exposed in their environment. Environment does not determine temperament but it can influence development by accenting strengths or weaknesses. A person is always responsible for the choices they make, regardless of their environment. The following variables can have influence over the development of a person's natural traits or tendencies.

GENDER

Males and females are motivated, in part, by different needs. These different needs may cause a different response to his or her environment.

WHERE YOU WERE REARED

The geographical location in the USA or foreign country where a person is reared may have influence on what one thinks is right, good, and normal.

WHEN YOU WERE REARED

Each decade seems to have a unique set of issues that tends to exert influence upon individual development. These issues help form beliefs and values.

EARLY HOME ENVIRONMENT

Every person needs consistent love, discipline, and praise. We do not need to be compared, condemned or criticized, which may have an adverse effect on the development of a healthy self-concept. An important issue in the early development of an individual is the match between a child's temperament and the expectations of the parents. Stella Chess and Alexander Thomas discuss this concept in their book, *Know Your Child*.

> We have called this general principle 'goodness or poorness of fit.' Goodness of fit exists when the demands and expectations of the parents and other people important to the child's life are compatible with the child's temperament, abilities and other characteristics. With such a fit, healthy development for the child can be expected. Poorness of fit, on the other hand, exists when demands and expectations are excessive and not compatible with the child's temperament, abilities and other characteristics. With such a fit, the child is likely to experience excessive stress, and healthy development is jeopardized. A child with a slow-to-warm-up temperament requires time and a number of exposures to a new situation before she can become an active, comfortable participant. But it is essential for such a child, as for all children, to develop the social competence to adapt to all new kinds of strange settings and experiences. If the parents and teachers recognize the child's temperament when the child first starts nursery school at four years, and if they do not pressure her into immediate involvement in the group

but let her move at her own pace from the periphery of the group to full participation, there is a good fit. Parents and teachers have made a demand that is within the youngster's ability to fulfill. Nursery school, for this child, will become an enjoyable and stimulating experience. This concept is likewise important for a child that eagerly wants to participate in a group activity. If the child is held back due to the expectations of the parent or others, it might also have an adverse effect on the child's development. The point is that it is important to identify the temperament needs of a young child and create a suitable environment.

GROUPS

In general, beliefs and values are developed from association and identification with schools, churches, clubs, etc.

PEERS

Those we associate with tend to have strong influence upon the establishment and development of our beliefs and value system, especially in the teen years.

EDUCATION

It is not just the amount of education obtained, but which schools were attended that is important. Educational institutions differ widely in beliefs and values.

WORK ETHIC

Having a work ethic means that a person places a positive value on applying themselves and doing a good job. If a person acquires a work ethic early in life, they will use their natural tendencies more productively. If not, the individual will have difficulty applying themselves effectively to whatever they decide to do in life.

PURPOSE

To get the most enjoyment out of life, a person needs to have a clearly defined purpose for living. Without a clear purpose, daily living can be tedious and empty. Fulfillment in life is not achieved because one is smarter, better looking, or even luckier than others. Purpose represents what inspires and fulfills you; it is your reason for getting out of bed every morning. The most fulfilled people have a clear purpose and specific, clearly defined goals.

NINE | TEMPERAMENT BLENDING CAUSES AN INNER FORCE THAT PUSHES AND PULLS

This principle enables us to understand the dynamics that occur when the various temperaments are combined.

All temperament blend combinations experience internal conflict on some level. The nature of the conflict is that two temperaments representing two different or opposing forces are at work at the same time, essentially pushing and pulling the person in two different directions. One temperament will push on the individual to act, and at the same time, the other will pull the individual back from acting. This produces internal tension. For most of the blends, the internal conflict or tension is not a major issue. There are a few of the blends, however, where the push/pull causes a more serious level of internal conflict and tension.

THE CHOLERIC | HIGH D BLENDS

A combination of Choleric and Sanguine or Choleric and Phlegmatic tendencies tend not to produce much internal conflict. The Choleric and Sanguine tendencies are both extroverted, active, and push outward. Internal tension occurs on occasion when the Choleric's need for results conflicts with the Sanguine's need for being with people. There is also not much internal conflict when the Choleric combines with the Phlegmatic temperament, because the Phlegmatic part is passive and offers no resistance to the Choleric tendencies (other than slowing him/her down a little). However, internal tension may arise when the Choleric's need for results meets the Phlegmatic's need to accommodate people.

Internal conflict (push/pull) occurs when the Choleric and Melancholy are blended together. The Choleric part wants to act first but the Melancholy part wants to plan first, producing tension. Both tendencies are focused on accomplishing the task. The Choleric part, however, wants the results quickly, while the Melancholy part wants the right results. If the individual learns to control both so that they plan first and then act, the internal conflict is greatly reduced, and this person will be focused and productive. When this is not managed well, there is instability and frequent displays of frustration.

THE SANGUINE | HIGH I BLENDS

There is not much conflict experienced when the Sanguine and Choleric are combined because both are extroverted, active and push outward and forward. Internal tension occurs on occasion when the Sanguine's need for being with people conflicts with the Choleric's need for results. The Sanguine and Phlegmatic in combination produce very little conflict because the Phlegmatic is passive and offers no internal resistance. Also, the Sanguine and the Phlegmatic are both people oriented. The Sanguine likes groups, and the Phlegmatic likes one-on-one relationships. Significant conflict always occurs when the Sanguine and Melancholy are combined. The Sanguine part is impulsive, active, and social, whereas the Melancholy part likes to plan and is private. Internal tension occurs when these two opposing forces try to control the person's behavior at the same time. Nervousness, high anxiety, and mood swings will likely occur if the individual does not control the push/pull of these temperament tendencies.

THE PHLEGMATIC | HIGH S BLENDS

When the Phlegmatic is the first temperament in combination with the other three, there is generally not much internal conflict. The Phlegmatic tendency has a calming effect on whatever temperament is second. There is, however, more internal conflict when the Phlegmatic is in combination with the Choleric, because the Phlegmatic part will resist the push of the Choleric tendencies, thus causing the tension. The Phlegmatic and Sanguine temperaments tend to work well together, although there is some conflict produced by the push of the Sanguine part on the Phlegmatic's passive tendency and the Phlegmatic's desire to move at a slower pace.

THE MELANCHOLY | HIGH C BLENDS

The greatest internal conflict from the Melancholy blends comes from the Melancholy-Choleric combination. These two tend to really annoy each other. The primary temperament Melancholy wants to think in great detail, while the Choleric part just wants results, now! These two tend to have a push/pull war going on most all of the time. The Melancholy-Sanguine blend tends to have some tension when the Melancholy part wants to be alone and the Sanguine part wants to be with people. The Melancholy-Phlegmatic blend tends to work well together with very little internal tension. The Melancholy part wants privacy, and that is okay with the Phlegmatic part.

SUMMARY

As you can see, there are different dynamics that occur as the various temperaments are combined. Sometimes there is great internal conflict (push/pull) when two temperaments attempt to influence behavior at the same time. One's task is to learn to control and direct the push/pull to minimize or eliminate the tension.

SUMMARY

CHAPTER **FOUR**

FREQUENTLY ASKED QUESTIONS

WHAT IS TEMPERAMENT?

TEMPERAMENT IS NOT THE SAME AS CHARACTER

Temperament has nothing to do with a person's character or their level of maturity. Character reflects the choices that are made.

TEMPERAMENT IS NOT THE SAME AS PERSONALITY

There are many factors that make up the total personality of a person. Temperament is only one of the many parts. Stella Chess and Alexander Thomas comment in their book, *Know Your Child*, 1987:

> But this recognition of the importance of temperament should not lead to an attempt to equate temperament with personality. We consider personality to be a composite of the enduring psychological attributes that constitute the unique individuality of a person. Personality structure is formed from the many diverse elements that shape psychological development, all acting together: motivations, abilities, interest, temperament, goals and value systems, psychological defense mechanisms, and the impact of the family

and the larger sociocultural environment. Temperament is one of the important factors that helps to shape personality, and its influence varies from person to person. Because temperamental categories or patterns evidence themselves as responses to environmental events and attitudes, the final results of such interactions vary from one person to another. In some instances, one temperamental attribute or pattern may be important in personality development, in other cases a different temperamental attribute may be significant, in still other cases the important temperament pattern may be different again.

TEMPERAMENT IS NOT A TYPE

A distinction needs to be made between a type and a trait. Types are broad categories, such as extrovert or introvert. Traits are more narrow and specific characteristics of behavior, such as being direct, sociable, patient or analytical.

The temperament model does not embrace the type approach to behavior. Rather, the temperament model recognizes that people are born with a cluster of traits which allows for different degrees of expression or development by an individual. Gordon Allport (1937), one of the founding figures of personality who focuses on trait psychology, says, "A man can be said to have a trait; but he cannot be said to have a type, rather he fits a type" (p. 296).

TEMPERAMENT REPRESENTS A CLUSTER OF TRAITS

Temperament is a cluster of inborn traits that causes you, in part, to do what you do, naturally. Temperament, therefore, represents the core foundational tendencies that make up an individual.

The four temperaments are represented by four distinct groups of traits or tendencies. Each cluster of traits produces a distinct manner of behavior that is different from the other groups. For example, the Choleric is result-oriented, the Sanguine is people-oriented, the Phlegmatic is service-oriented, and the Melancholy is quality-oriented.

Each trait can be placed on a continuum from low expression to high expression. For example, one may possess the trait of being social to a high degree, moderate degree, or almost not at all. A trait is like a rheostat switch that controls a light. When you turn the switch up the light gets brighter, when you turn the switch down the lights gets dimmer. The more of a given trait one possess, the more observable it will be in their behavior.

The temperament model embraces the trait approach, which allows for a particular trait to be possessed and developed to varying degrees. Temperament, therefore, represents natural traits or tendencies with which a person is born. How well these natural traits are developed depends on the individual's desire and motivation. A person's work ethic, purpose and passion in life are also important factors in the degree to which traits or tendencies benefit the individual. Arnold Buss and Robert Plomin (1975) give Gordon Allport's definition of temperament in *A Temperament Theory of Personality Development*:

> Temperament refers to the characteristic phenomena of an individual's nature, including his susceptibility to emotional stimulation, his customary strength and speed of response, the quality of his prevailing mood, and all the peculiarities of fluctuation and intensity of mood, these being phenomena regarded as dependent on constitutional makeup, and therefore largely hereditary in origin.

John Geier (1983), in the *The Child's Profile: Library of Classical Patterns*, describes temperament this way:

> During a lifetime we experience many emotions, but there is an emotional state which is most characteristic for each of us. We depart from that basic temperament when aroused by such feelings as love, hate, sadness, anger, rage, or exuberance. However, these emotions tend to be as transient as they are intense. Love slips through our fingers; hate is difficult to sustain for long periods; joy and sorrow eventually dissipate. Like strong winds, these emotions temporarily ruffle the surface of our usual emotional demeanor. When others describe us with such words as friendly, logical, aggressive, or careful, they are referring to the feeling state we usually project. That state reflects our self-concept and has evolved from genetic predispositions and the shaping forces of the environment. Others may approve or disapprove of our temperament. It may meld or conflict with the expectations of groups or organizations. The crucial aspect is recognizing the 'given' of our emotions and choosing the environment in which we will be accepted and productive.

TEMPERAMENT IS WHAT A PERSON IS MOST OF THE TIME

Temperament represents the way a person relates to others and responds to events. It is what you have observed and expect someone's behavior to be, most of the time.

Have you ever referred to someone as shy or outgoing? Without realizing it, you were referring to certain temperament traits. These traits are what you know and expect the person to be every time you are with them. Thus, temperament behavior is, for the most part, predictable. The exception being when one temporarily experiences strong emotions, such as anger or fear, or is trying to deceive another. Actually, acting is a form of acceptable deception. A person is knowingly acting like they are someone else. Unfortunately, some purposely act like someone they are not in order to deceive.

Society would simply not be able to exist if behavior were not predictable. Imagine what life would be like if everyone were different every time you met them. Imagine the chaos. Without consistency in people, without predictability, society simply would not survive.

TEMPERAMENT IS A FORCE

Temperament is a force within that represents various traits or tendencies that produce an urge, drive, and appetite. Temperament urges and even drives a person to act in a particular manner. Temperament, as an appetite or void, requires satisfaction. An obvious illustration is when you are hungry, you have a need to eat; a void to be satisfied. When you eat, the void is filled and you are satisfied and no longer hungry. Temperament is that way. It pushes or urges you to behave according to the tendencies that represent your temperament blend. For example, there are those who are natural people-people. They enjoy being with, around or just standing by others. They like to talk, have fun and be active with others. There is a force within these people that urges them to do this. Ask those with the Sanguine temperament and they will tell you, "I just like being with people." Conversely, there are those who are private in nature and they prefer not to be with, around or by others. There is an equal force within them that urges them to avoid contact with others. Both are normal and both have a force inside that pushes them according to their natural temperament tendencies.

TEMPERAMENT IS A NEED

Abraham Maslow says that a need is something that, if you do not meet, makes you sick. Air, food and water are physical needs without which a person would become ill and, of course, die. Temperament represents needs, but no one will die without these needs being met. A temperament need represents what is important and highly desirable in the core of an individual. Temperament is a need that urges, drives and motivates a person to act according to his natural tendencies. If temperament needs are not met, the individual will not feel at peace or function efficiently. Meeting temperament needs is, therefore, critical to a person's sense of well-being and feeling of self-worth.

Let's again use the Sanguine temperament as an example. As a people-person, the Sanguine enjoys social involvement. This includes talking to others or just being in the presence of one or more people. Social contact is a need of the Sanguine temperament, and if not met, the person will not feel okay about themselves. This is just one of the four temperaments. The others will have specific needs as does this one, but all will be different from each other. The Choleric, for example, needs to see results quickly; the Phlegmatic needs to follow a routine; the Melancholy needs to have a detailed plan. These needs are both normal and natural. Everyone, therefore, should provide adequate satisfaction for their temperament needs in order to be at their best.

WHAT IS THE ORIGIN OF TEMPERAMENT?

There are two possibilities. Either people are born without natural tendencies, or they are born with natural tendencies.

PEOPLE ARE BORN WITHOUT NATURAL TENDENCIES

Some believe that people start life as a blank slate (referred to as tabula rasa) and that the environment determines the personality. Dr. James Dobson (1987) is not in favor of this position but reports it in *Parenting Isn't for Cowards*:

> Sigmund Freud, the father of Psychoanalysis, and J.B. Watson, the creator of behaviorism, believed that newborns come into the world as 'blank slates' on which the environment would later write. For them a baby had no inborn characteristics of personality that distinguished him from other infants. Everything he would become, both good and evil, would result from the experiences to be provided by the world around him. He could make no independent decisions because he had no real freedom of choice...no ability to consider his circumstances and to act rationally on them. Watson even rejected the existence of a mind...

The view that tendencies are acquired is also stated by David Merrill and Roger Reid (1981) in *Personal Styles & Effective Performance*:

> "Why do people develop these behavioral preferences? ...people tend to do those things that make them feel comfortable. Once a pattern of actions receives positive reinforcement, we have a tendency to repeat it."

PEOPLE ARE BORN WITH NATURAL TENDENCIES

This position teaches that a person is born with natural tendencies and that these are developed according to that person's response to their environment. In the article "Born to be Shy?" Jules Asher (1987) wrote the following concerning Dr. Jerome Kagan's research:

> We've all met shy toddlers—the ones who cling to their parents and only reluctantly venture into an unfamiliar room. Faced with strangers, they first freeze, falling silent and staring at them. They seem visibly tense until they've had a chance to size up the new scene. Parents of such children are likely to say they've always been on the timid side. 'It's just his way,' one might say.

Arnold Buss and Robert Plomin (1975) discuss this position in their book, *A Temperament Theory of Personality Development*:

> To aid understanding, we shall start with a non temperament model of personality. This model assumes that each person starts as a blank slate (tabula rasa) that will be written on by experience. It assumes that man's nature is that he has no nature. It flatly rejects the possibility of inborn tendencies that determine individual differences in personality. Environment is all. If there are stable individual differences, they are learned individual differences, they are learned during childhood, during adulthood, or both. We have no quarrel with this model if it is restricted to some aspects of personality. There is presently no basis for assuming that differences among persons in self-esteem, guilt, or authoritarianism are derived from inborn dispositions. These and many other aspects of personality would seem to be wholly acquired during the course of living. But we cannot accept this model for all aspects of personality. Some behavioral tendencies—we would argue, some of the most basic personality tendencies—originate in inherited dispositions.

Dr. James Dobson (1987) discusses temperaments in his book, *Parenting Isn't for Cowards*:

> It is my supposition that these temperaments are prepackaged before birth and do not have to be cultivated or encouraged. They will make themselves known soon enough. Behavioral scientists are now observing and documenting

the subtle understandings that have been evident in Scriptures for thousands of years. One of the most ambitious of these efforts to study temperaments of babies has been in progress for more than three decades. It is known as the York Longitudinal Study, 1969. The findings from this investigation, led by psychiatrists Stella Chess and Alexander Thomas, are now reported in their excellent book for parents entitled, *Know Your Child.* To my delight, Chess and Thomas found that babies not only differ significantly from one another at the moment of birth, but those differences tend to be rather persistent throughout childhood.

In their book *Personality Structure & Measurement*, Dr. Hans Eysenck and Sybil Eysenck (1969) state that traits are rooted in genetics:

These early ideas developed by Greek writers, thinkers and physicians already contain, if only in embryo, the three main notions which characterize modern work in personality. In the first place, behavior or conduct is to be described in terms of traits which characterize given individuals in varying degrees. In the second place, these traits cohere or correlate and define certain more fundamental and more all-embracing types. In the third place, these types are essentially based on constitutional, genetic or inborn factors, which are to be discovered in the physiological, neurological and biochemical structure of the individual.

Dr. Tim LaHaye (1977), in *Understanding the Male Temperament*, says, "The combination of inherited traits he receives from his parents at the time of conception will determine his eventual temperament."

Finally, perhaps the best proof of all is to ask a mother who has raised at least two children. She will likely tell you that they were different from birth. My daughter has twin girls and knew before they were born that one was going to be active and the other one was going to be laid-back, and that is exactly how they are today.

WILL MY TEMPERAMENT BLEND EVER CHANGE?

No. The temperament blend you were born with remains throughout your life-span. Some are confused about this. They think that because they have experienced some growth, their temperament blend has somehow changed. All that has really happened is that they have learned self-control and have matured. There are three areas to consider:

TEMPORARY MODIFICATION

There are times when your behavior does not represent your temperament blend, but this will always be temporary. A situation may require that you behave in a way that is not natural for you to act, but when the need has passed, you will once again behave in a way that represents your temperament blend. For example, if you are a Phlegmatic-Melancholy and the Choleric temperament is your least, you may become assertive if a situation requires you to do so. After the moment has passed, you will once again be pleasant and accommodating.

GROWTH

Some report that their temperament has changed over the years (e.g., once shy and now outgoing). I have found this to always be a person with a combination of an extroverted and introverted temperament like the Choleric-Phlegmatic or the Sanguine-Melancholy.

There is a way of behaving that you feel is right, good, and normal. This represents your temperamental comfort zone of behavior. When people suggest that their temperament has changed, that usually means that due to circumstances in their early years, they did not function out of their primary temperament. Most often they had a domineering caregiver that would not allow them the freedom to be themselves. They essentially hid in the safety of their second temperament. After growing, aging, and getting away from the negative influence, they settled into expressing their primary temperament tendencies.

We are all influenced by many variables, such as the quality of early home life, education, travel, etc. Regardless of these early influences, as individuals develop, they begin to feel more comfortable with the way they want to be, and are willing to actually behave in that manner. It is not that their temperament has changed, it is simply that they are now expressing the behavior they have always wanted to express. They are in their temperamental comfort zone.

PERMANENT MODIFICATION

It is possible to control your natural tendencies so that your behavior is modified and does not reflect a particular weakness. For example, the Sanguine has a tendency to talk a lot. Until they learn to moderate the need to verbalize, it can, at times, be annoying to others. Once they become aware of this weakness, they can decide to not talk as much, thus gaining control over this weakness. Each temperament has natural weaknesses that need to be controlled: the Choleric can be too result-oriented at the expense of others, the Phlegmatic can be too routine and refuse to change, the Melancholy can be negative and too rigid.

CAN ANYONE BE A LEADER REGARDLESS OF THEIR TEMPERAMENT?

Yes. A person will lead based on their temperament. The Choleric and Sanguine will lead by directing. They will tell you to get a task completed. The Phlegmatic and Melancholy will lead by example. They will show you how to complete the task. Each one will be effective in their own way. Consider the following Presidents of the United States: Lyndon Johnson, Choleric; Ronald Reagan, Sanguine; Gerald Ford, Phlegmatic; George W. Bush, Melancholy.

To be a more well-balanced leader, one must be aware of the potential that a strength may become a weakness if overextended. For example, the Choleric can push people too hard for results; the Sanguine may become too friendly with those they lead; the Phlegmatic may be so routine that they resists any kind of change; and the Melancholy may develop such a detailed plan that it does not allow for flexibility or creativity.

WHAT ARE THE BEST TERMS TO USE FOR THE TEMPERAMENTS?

My personal preference is to use the most traditional terms when referring to the four temperaments: Choleric, Sanguine, Phlegmatic, and Melancholy. This, of course, is a matter of opinion.

A descriptive term only suggests what the person may do in certain situations; it does not represent the essence of the temperament. Using the traditional terms encourages the investigation into what each term represents, which allows for a more complete understanding of what it means to be that particular temperament. The point is that a term should not limit understanding or label a temperament with a narrow description.

For example, a common term used to refer to the Choleric is Dominant. The Choleric can be dominant, but they are not dominant all the time. The term limits our understanding of the Choleric temperament. A common term used to refer to the Sanguine is Expressive. Indeed, they can be expressive, but they will not be expressive all the time. The term limits our understanding of the Sanguine temperament. A common term used to refer to the Phlegmatic is Amiable. It is true that they can be amiable, but it is also true that they can stubbornly resist being cooperative. The term limits our understanding of the Phlegmatic temperament. A common term used to refer to the Melancholy is Compliance, suggesting that they will always be this way. It is true that they can be compliant, but this is true only if they respect the authority. The term limits our understanding of the Melancholy temperament.

The most popular terms used today are High D (Choleric), High I (Sanguine), High S (Phlegmatic) and High C (Melancholy). Because these terms are widely recognized, they are included throughout this work.

HOW DO THE DIFFERENT TEMPERAMENT NAMES CORRELATE?

There have been many different terms used to refer to the four temperaments. I have collected over twenty names for each of the four temperaments. See Figure 3 for a correlation of some of the more popular terms.

TEMPERAMENT NAME CORRELATIONS
FIGURE 3

CHOLERIC	SANGUINE	PHLEGMATIC	MELANCHOLY
Dominant	Influencing	Steadiness	Compliance
High D	High I	High S	High C
Driver	Expressive	Amiable	Analytical
Director	Socializer	Relater	Thinker
Red	Yellow	Gray	Blue
*NF	*SP	*NT	*SJ

*Myers-Briggs Type Indicator

WHAT IS MY TEMPERAMENT BLEND AND PATTERN?

To identify your temperament blend, do the following: first, read through the fifteen pattern descriptions in chapters six through nine. Select the pattern with which you are the most comfortable—the one that you feel describes you best and that you are in at least 85% agreement. Be able to say, "That's me most of the time." The higher the level of agreement, the better. Be sure that you pick the one that you are and not the one that you want to be. Do not force yourself to agree with the blend that you have selected. When you read the blend that describes you, you will recognize that it is mostly accurate and correct. Remember, temperament is what you are most of the time; it is your most natural and comfortable way of behaving. Rate your response to each blend on a scale between 1 and 10 as illustrated below.

LIKE ME   10---9---8---7---6---5---4---3---2---1   NOT LIKE ME

WHAT ARE THE MOST COMMON TEMPERAMENTS?

My research began in the early 1970's and includes thousands of people. I have tracked the frequency of occurrence of the fifteen patterns. Although all fifteen patterns appear, not all appear at the same rate or frequency. Some patterns appear frequently while others appear much less frequently.

My research included giving and validating the DISC and the DISC II instruments in both the private and work environments, and giving seminars in churches. My research continued as a therapist.

The recurring frequency of the various patterns has been consistent. I have divided the occurrence of the patterns into the three following categories.

COMMON PATTERNS

These seven temperament blends and patterns occur most frequently (not in this order):

Choleric-Melancholy	D-C	Strategist
Sanguine-Phlegmatic	I-S	Relater
Sanguine-Melancholy	I-C	Performer
Phlegmatic-Sanguine	S-I	Harmonizer
Phlegmatic-Melancholy	S-C	Helper / Supporter
Melancholy-Sanguine	C-I	Diplomat
Melancholy-Phlegmatic	C-S	Analyst

SOMEWHAT COMMON PATTERNS

These three temperament blends and patterns occur less frequently than those listed in the previous page (not in this order):

Sanguine-Choleric	I-D	Negotiator & Marketer
Melancholy-Choleric	C-D	Trainer
Melancholy-Phlegmatic-Choleric	C-S-D	Idealist

LEAST COMMON PATTERNS

These three temperament blends and patterns occur the least frequent (not in this order):

Choleric-Sanguine	D-I	Executive & Motivator
Choleric-Phlegmatic	D-S	Director
Phlegmatic-Choleric	S-D	Inspector

There will be a high concentration of a particular temperament blend or pattern in a specific environment. For example, in a sales organization you would expect to find mostly the Sanguine temperament. I worked with one sales organization for seven years and they had salespeople across the country. I validated the temperament patterns of the entire nationwide sales force and the breakdown was as follows: 75 % were Sanguine, 15% were Choleric, 5% were Phlegmatic, and 5% were Melancholy. I worked with a group of economists at a Federal Bank and they were almost all Melancholy. So, a particular environment will usually attract a high number of a particular temperament.

NOTE | As you will see in the following chapters, there are several temperament blends with two patterns. For example, the Choleric-Sanguine (D-I) has two expressions; the Executive and Motivational patterns. The two represent the different levels of blend intensity. Below is a list of all the blends which have more than one expression:

Choleric-Sanguine	D-I	Executive & Motivator
Sanguine-Choleric	I-D	Negotiator & Marketer
Melancholy-Choleric	C-D	Trainer & Idealist

ARE TEMPERAMENTS THE SAME IN OTHER CULTURES?

Yes. Remember that Hippocrates (470-360 B.C.) is given credit for identifying the temperament concept about 2,400 years ago. He made his observations in the Greek culture. The concept, however, is rooted in the ancient Chinese predating Hippocrates.

It was true of people then and it is true of people today, everyone has a temperament. Everyone has a blend of the four temperaments regardless of their culture or ethnic origin. I have interviewed people from many countries such as China, Germany, Indonesia, Vietnam, Mexico, and Australia to name a few.

IS "SUPINE" A FIFTH TEMPERAMENT?

1994 National Christian Counselors Association (NCCA) founders Drs. Richard and Phyllis Arno claimed to have discovered a fifth temperament; Supine (Arno, 2008, p. 118). In the book, *The Missing Link, Revealing Spiritual Genetics*, Richard Gene Arno suggests that there needs to be a fifth temperament because there are behavioral traits that simply could not fit within the currently existing temperaments (p. 118). Supines "wants and needs social acceptance very much" (p. 120), "...no other temperament keeps and follows 'the rules' any more than the Supine" (p. 121), "...extreme weak-willed, wanting to say "no" but not knowing how" (p. 122).

The reason that Arno may have felt the need to identify a fifth temperament is the common practice of simply using primary temperaments without taking into account the influence of the secondary temperament. If you look at the descriptions of the different Supine traits you will notice that they are the expression of the Sanguine (High I) and Melancholy (High C) temperament blend, known as the Performer Pattern (see page 100 for the detailed description of this temperament blend).

WHAT TEMPERAMENT BLENDS ARE LIKELY TO MARRY?

There is no rhyme or reason why two people have chemistry, connect, communicate well and live happily ever after. There is no known formula to make it happen, it just happens. People are attracted to each other for a wide variety of reasons, sometimes it works and sometimes it doesn't! Attraction to another person is a mystery and it's one of the reasons life is exciting.

During my years of using the temperament model as a consultant and therapist, I compiled the marriage choices of 315 people identifying the twelve temperament blends. The breakdown of the 315 individuals is as follows: 51 were Choleric; 109 were Sanguine; 85 were Phlegmatic; and 70 were Melancholy. Their marriage choices are in the following charts.

CHOLERIC | HIGH D

The study included 51 Cholerics. They made the following choices in a mate:

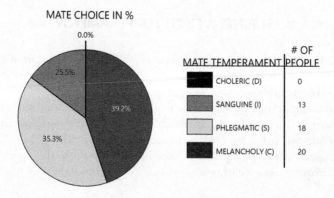

MATE CHOICE IN %

MATE TEMPERAMENT	# OF PEOPLE
CHOLERIC (D)	0
SANGUINE (I)	13
PHLEGMATIC (S)	18
MELANCHOLY (C)	20

I did not find a Choleric married or engaged to another Choleric. This is of no surprise since the Choleric has such strong ego strength that it would be nearly impossible for these two to live at peace with each other.

The extroverted Choleric chose an introverted temperament 75% of the time. Perhaps this was to compliment their temperament tendencies so they would not be in competition with their need for control.

SANGUINE | HIGH I

The study included 109 Sanguines. They made the following choices in a mate

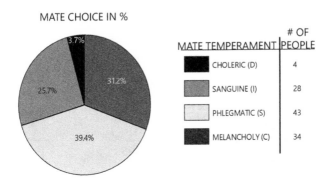

MATE CHOICE IN %

MATE TEMPERAMENT	# OF PEOPLE
CHOLERIC (D)	4
SANGUINE (I)	28
PHLEGMATIC (S)	43
MELANCHOLY (C)	34

The extroverted Sanguine selected an introverted temperament 70% of the time. Perhaps this was to compliment their temperament tendencies and not be in competition with their need for attention.

PHLEGMATIC | HIGH S

The study included 85 Phlegmatics. They made the following choices in a mate:

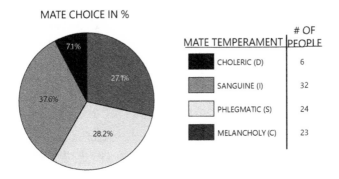

MATE CHOICE IN %

MATE TEMPERAMENT	# OF PEOPLE
CHOLERIC (D)	6
SANGUINE (I)	32
PHLEGMATIC (S)	24
MELANCHOLY (C)	23

The introverted Phlegmatic married an opposite temperament 45% of the time and they married a similar temperament, 55% of the time. The Phlegmatic is slightly more likely to marry a similar temperament perhaps revealing a desire for a more stable and peaceful relationship.

MELANCHOLY | HIGH C

The study included 70 Melancholies. They made the following choices in a mate:

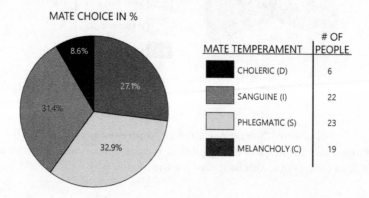

MATE CHOICE IN %

MATE TEMPERAMENT	# OF PEOPLE
CHOLERIC (D)	6
SANGUINE (I)	22
PHLEGMATIC (S)	23
MELANCHOLY (C)	19

The introverted Melancholy married an opposite temperament 40% of the time and a similar temperament 60 % of the time.

When an extrovert (Choleric or Sanguine) selected a mate they selected an introvert mostly—a combined 72.55% of the time. However, when an introvert (Phlegmatic or Melancholy) selected a mate they selected another introvert mostly—a combined 57.5% of the time. So, in this study, an extrovert is more like to marry an opposite than an introvert. Compiling a larger number of couples may render different results

MARITAL SATISFACTION

The purpose of my study was not to determine the level of satisfaction experienced by these married couples. Much has been written suggesting the requirements for a happy and fulfilling marriage.

My view is that it takes two people who want to be in the relationship, who

MATE SELECTION BY TEMPERAMENT BLEND

			CHOLERIC BLEND			SANGUINE BLEND			PHLEGMATIC BLEND			MELANCHOLY BLEND		
			D-I	D-S	D-C	I-D	I-S	I-C	S-D	S-I	S-C	C-D	C-I	C-S
CHOLERIC BLEND		D-I	–	–	–	1	–	1	–	1	1	1	–	1
		D-S	–	–	–	–	–	–	–	–	–	–	1	2
		D-C	–	–	–	–	2	–	1	1	2	–	–	1
SANGUINE BLEND		I-D	–	–	1	4	3	1	–	1	3	–	–	9
		I-S	1	2	3	3	4	3	–	6	8	2	2	5
		I-C	2	1	3	3	5	2	1	5	8	–	–	4
PHLEGMATIC BLEND		S-D	–	–	2	3	–	–	–	–	0	1	1	–
		S-I	4	–	5	5	7	15	–	5	7	1	2	5
		S-C	1	1	5	7	3	3	1	5	6	5	2	6
MELANCHOLY BLEND		C-D	2	–	–	0	2	1	–	2	1	–	–	–
		C-I	2	2	3	2	2	5	1	3	5	5	1	5
		C-S	6	1	4	8	5	9	1	5	5	1	3	4
		Total	18	7	26	38	33	40	5	34	45	16	12	42

are committed to each other, and they are willing to work on the relationship as it evolves. It is best that their view of the world is unfolding at the same time. They not only love each other but they also like each other and enjoy being together. They are involved in the maturing process together and are more similar than not. Similarities facilitate happy coexistence because there is less cause for potential disagreements. It is especially important to have a similar work ethic. Mutual respect, heart-to-heart communication, connection and chemistry are essential. A willingness to forgive and compromise are foundational.

I did, however, observe what appeared to be a natural temperament match that produced a high level of marital satisfaction, naturally. There appears to be a special attraction and a natural compliment between the following pairs:

Sanguine-Melancholy (I-C) & Phlegmatic-Sanguine (S-I)
Sanguine-Phlegmatic (I-S) & Melancholy-Sanguine (C-I)
Sanguine-Phlegmatic (I-S) & Melancholy-Phlegmatic (C-S)
Choleric-Melancholy (D-C) & Melancholy-Phlegmatic (C-S)

POTENTIAL MARITAL DISSATISFACTION

I also found one match that almost always produces a high level of conflict and dissatisfaction. As a therapist, I have counseled more couples that were both Sanguine-Melancholy (I-C) than any other combination. The reason is that this blend has a high need for attention and they are too sensitive to the possibility of being embarrassed or rejected.

In general, when two extroverts marry with strong, expressive temperaments, the potential for conflict will rise. When two introverts marry it decreases the potential for conflict because they are naturally less assertive, more compliant, and more accommodating to the needs of their mate.

Please keep in mind that these are generalizations and not absolutes. Any two people, regardless of their temperament, can live in harmony with each other if they are willing to do so. Likewise, any two people, regardless of their temperament, may decide to live in disharmony.

ADJUSTMENTS ARE NECESSARY

If you live with another person, adjustments are going to be necessary for a satisfying, peaceful coexistence. The temperaments give insights into the adjustments needed. For example, if married to a Choleric you have to tolerate and adjust to their need to be in control of, well, everything. The Choleric must reduce their need to be in control. If married to a Sanguine you need to tolerate and adjust to the Sanguine's need to talk and be the center of attention. The Sanguine must reduce their need to talk and be the center of everything. If married to a Phlegmatic you need to tolerate and adjust to their adherence to a routine and a lack of a sense of urgency. The Phlegmatic must develop a willingness to change their routine and not procrastinate. If married to a Melancholy you need to tolerate and adjust to their need for a plan and privacy. The Melancholy must be willing to change their plan and be more sociable.

The degree to which one is willing to adjust to the needs of their mate and their own needs is paramount to whether or not marital satisfaction may be achieved. A word of caution: what attracts you to another person may eventually repel you if you do not adjust to the other person's temperament tendencies. Without adjusting, the potential for building resentment increases dramatically.

WHAT JOBS MATCH MY TEMPERAMENT?

This is not an easy question to answer because people are drawn to various types of work for different reasons. Whatever job you are drawn to, however, will be performed using your natural temperament tendencies.

All of the temperament blends perform well in various sales jobs. The Choleric will naturally seek sales jobs that produce results quickly and will sell a product that offers big financial rewards. The Sanguine likes being with people so they will do the best in all types of sales jobs. The Phlegmatic and Melancholy will seek low-pressure sales positions so they will not have to push to get the order. The Phlegmatic is the best at being a route salesperson because they like to follow a routine. The Melancholy will naturally seek a sales position of a technical nature so they can apply their detail knowledge of the product.

The highest level of motivation is achieved when you match your natural tendencies to the requirements of the task. Below are potential career choices for each temperament based on their natural tendencies.

CHOLERIC | HIGH D

Cholerics will be the most productive in a career that allows them to get results quickly and be in a position to influence and direct others. The Choleric is often found in the following positions: owner, president, CEO, top management, attorney, entrepreneur, sales, sales manager, real estate developer, and project manager.

SANGUINE | HIGH I

The Sanguine will be the most productive in a career that allows them to work with and influence others. The Sanguine is often found in the following positions: owner, president, CEO, top management, attorney, entrepreneur, sales, sales manager, real estate developer, project manager, public relations, human resources, entertainment, etc.

The Sanguine-Melancholy (Performer Pattern: I-C) has a wide range of ability and is naturally attracted to careers, such as: the performing arts (acting, singing, and dancing), teacher, writer, graphic artist, interior decorator, and talk-show host.

PHLEGMATIC | HIGH S

The Phlegmatic will be the most productive in a career that allows them to have a routine and to be of service to others. The Phlegmatic is often found in the following positions: customer service, nurse, teacher, mid-level management, pharmaceutical salesperson, sales clerk, route salesperson, operating a postal route, and office staff worker.

MELANCHOLY | HIGH C

The Melancholy will be the most productive in a career that allows them to do detail work. The Melancholy is often found in the following positions: bookkeeper, accountant, engineer, pharmacist, technician, computer programmer, musician, writer, artist, and technical sales.

Remember, you will be the most content and productive in a career that matches your natural temperament needs and tendencies.

IS THERE A RELATIONSHIP BETWEEN BODY TYPES AND TEMPERAMENTS?

Yes. There is evidence that there is a correlation between a person's body type and their temperament.

In the 1940s, psychologist Dr. William Sheldon (1898-1977) suggested that there are three basic body types, called somatotypes (based on the three tissue layers: endoderm, mesoderm, and ectoderm). He taught that these body types are associated with personality characteristics, representing a correlation between physique and temperament. Dr. Sheldon and others have identified the following three somatotypes and related personality traits. These observations grouped the Choleric and Sanguine with a similar body type and the Phlegmatic and Melancholy with distinctively different body types.

MESOMORPHIC BODY TYPE | CHOLERIC (HIGH D) & SANGUINE (HIGH I)

The mesomorphic body type is hard and muscular, it has a mature appearance, rectangular shape, thick skin, and has an upright posture. The personality traits associated with the mesomorph include being adventurous, having a desire for power and dominance, being courageous, being indifferent to what others think or want, being assertive and bold, having a zest for physical activity, being competitive, and having a desire for risk and chance.

ENDOMORPHIC BODY TYPE | PHLEGMATIC (HIGH S)

The endomorphic body type is soft with underdeveloped muscles, has a round shape and an overdeveloped digestive system. The personality traits associated with the endomorph include being tolerant, possessing an evenness of emotions, having a love of comfort, being sociable and good humored, being relaxed, having a need for affection, and a love for food.

ECTOMORPHIC BODY TYPE | MELANCHOLY (HIGH C)

The ectomorphic body type is thin with a flat chest, delicate build, young appearance, tall, lightly muscled, stoop-shouldered, and has a large brain. The personality traits associated with the ectomorph include being self-conscious, preferring privacy, being introverted and inhibited, being socially anxious, being artistic and mentally intense, and being emotionally restrained.

The research that Dr. Sheldon did matches the temperament traits of the Phlegmatic and Melancholy. He grouped the Choleric and Sanguine temperament into one body type. However, the personality traits for the mesomorph body type are a better match for the Choleric than the Sanguine temperament. Both of these temperaments tend to have a more muscular, athletic body type. There are exceptions, of course, but this concept appears to be mostly accurate. The body type correlation with a temperament is not absolute but it is obvious that temperament affects a person's body type.

SUMMARY

You were born with your temperament blend and it will never change. For example, a Choleric-Sanguine will never become a Melancholy-Phlegmatic or any other temperament because it is impossible to change your temperament, just as it is impossible to change your basic body structure.

The conclusion is that you are normal. You have natural strengths and weaknesses and it is okay to be yourself. You do not have to pretend to be someone you are not. I am not suggesting that you always demonstrate the traits of your temperament or that it is permissible to overlook areas that you need to control. I am saying that it is not only possible, but it is necessary to control and modify your natural tendencies in order to become a more mature and well-balanced person.

Here are a few reasons why you should relax and enjoy being yourself: First, you are the most comfortable when you are behaving in a manner that represents the controlled strengths of your temperament. Second, you are perceived in the best possible way when you are expressing the controlled strengths of your temperament. Third, you have your most positive impact upon others when you are expressing the controlled strengths of your temperament. Relax, enjoy being who you are.

CHAPTER **FIVE**

PSYCHOLOGY, COUNSELING AND TEMPERAMENT

PSYCHOLOGY

The field of psychology gives superficial treatment to the concept of the temperaments. The subject is either not mentioned, mentioned a little, or written off as being too old or irrelevant. Perhaps the reason for not giving the temperament model of behavior serious consideration is because of a major debate in psychology over which has the most influence on behavior, nature or nurture.

Sir Francis Galton (1822–1911) wrote about distinguishing between the greater influence of heredity (nature) and environment (nurture) and coined these terms. The nature position, also referred to as nativism, is the view that certain skills or abilities are native or hard-wired into the brain prior to birth. The nurture position is that humans acquire all or almost all of their behavioral tendencies after birth and is referred to as *tabula rasa* (i.e., born as a blank slate).

The nature position supports the temperament model of behavior which teaches that an individual is born with traits or natural tendencies: people are born predisposed (hard-wired) to a way of thinking, feeling, and behaving. With pre-wired tendencies, the nature position holds that a person's personality is not determined by the environment. Rather, the individual responds to their environment based on their pre-wired temperament tendencies and develops their strengths and weaknesses (or not) accordingly. It follows, therefore, that an individual makes choices based on their predisposed way of thinking, feeling, and behaving. This is the temperament model of behavior.

The field of psychology holds almost exclusively to the nurture position believing that environmental influences have the greater impact in determining a person's personality and behavior. Nature is recognized as having only slight, if any, influence by some psychologists.

All agree that nurture is vitally important in the early environment of a child and may have great impact. However, just because a person was raised in a good environment or a bad environment does not guarantee that the person will follow their respective example, good or bad. My opinion is that the nurture position places too much emphasis on the environment in which the person is raised. It relieves and/or reduces the accountability and responsibility of the individual for the choices they make. This position makes it easy for people to blame others for their own behavior: "I am this way because my mother, father, brother, sister, aunt, uncle, friend, neighbor, dog, or cat did this or that to me!" The age in which we live encourages blaming everything and everyone else for one's bad behavior but the one behaving badly.

A basic, but overlooked, truth is that an individual makes choices in the environment in which they are reared. I have counseled people who have come from good environments and rebelled against their training. Likewise, I have counseled people who came from bad environments and decided not to follow the examples they were shown. We easily forget that human beings make their own choices, even a child. My conclusion is that it is not the environment that is most important, it is the person's response to their environment that is the most important. I am not suggesting that a care-giver's bad example is to be excused or minimized.

Dr. William Glasser (1999) wrote in *Choice Theory, A New Psychology of Personal Freedom*:

> Suppose you could ask all the people in the world who are not hungry, sick, or poor, people who seem to have a lot to live for, to give you an honest answer to the question, 'How are you?' Millions would say, 'I'm miserable.' If asked why, almost all of them would blame someone else for their misery—lovers, wives, husbands, exes, children, parents, teachers, students, or people they work with. There is hardly a person alive who hasn't been heard saying, 'You're driving me crazy. . . . That really upsets me. . . . Don't you have any consideration for how I feel? . . . You make me so mad, I can't see straight.' It never crosses their minds that they are choosing the misery they are complaining about.

> Choice theory explains that, for all practical purposes, we choose everything we do, including the misery we feel. Other people can neither make us miserable nor make us happy. All we can get from them or give to them is information. But by itself, information cannot make us do or feel anything. It goes into our brains where we process it and then decide what to do. As I explain in great detail in this book, we choose all our actions and thoughts and, indirectly, almost all our feelings and much of our physiology...Choice theory teaches we are much more indirectly, almost all our feelings and much of our physiology...Choice theory teaches we are much more in control of our lives than we realize.

I would add that we are more in control of our lives than we are *willing* to accept.

Perhaps the most powerful illustration I can offer that individuals are in control of their behavior and responsible for their choices, regardless of their environment or circumstances, comes from Victor Frankl, a Jewish psychiatrist. He and his family were imprisoned in a German concentration camp during WWII. Dr. Frankl's 1946 book, *Man's Search for Meaning* chronicles his experiences as a prisoner and describes his method of finding a reason to live. Dr. Frankl explained in one statement how he survived the unthinkable that he endured. He watched every member of his family die except his sister yet he made this statement: "Everything can be taken from a man or a woman but one thing: the last of human freedoms to choose one's attitude in any given set of circumstances, to choose one's own way."

A Sanguine will be a Sanguine no matter what their environment, good or bad. The environment will have impact (or not) on how the temperament is expressed but only to a point. Regardless of the environment, a person will express their temperament tendencies. Of course, we can engineer an example where someone under extreme conditions (like a concentration camp) behaved differently. However, once the moment has passed the person will again express their natural temperament tendencies.

To summarize, the temperament model of behavior teaches that people are born with natural tendencies. These natural tendencies are in the core of an individual representing natural drives and needs. An individual is born with their temperament already determined (hard-wired). The individual then responds to their environment according to their temperament drives and needs. Temperament is, therefore, the platform upon which an individual responds to people and events. This model teaches that we are responsible to use the associated strengths of our temperament, and overcome the natural weaknesses in order to live an effective and productive life. It's a choice.

NOTE | A temperament need represents what is important and highly desirable in the core of an individual. A need is a drive that urges one to behave in such a manner until it is fulfilled. Meeting temperament needs is critical to a person's feeling of self-worth and sense of value.

COUNSELING

Since the field of psychology rejects the relevance of the four temperaments, it is no surprise that the temperament model of behavior in counseling is also largely ignored. Some therapists do use the temperament model on some level but there is no major methodology in psychology or counseling that seriously considers this approach to explain behavior. When the concept is used it is mostly through The Myers-Briggs Type Indicator. As noted earlier, this instrument is not without controversy.

USING THE TEMPERAMENT MODEL OF BEHAVIOR

The temperament model of behavior teaches that everyone is born with natural tendencies which determines their level of emotion, speed of response, and natural approach to people and events. As noted earlier, this understanding has been around for at least 2,400 years, enduring the test of time.

The temperament model of behavior is the best tool I have used in my counseling practice. To make the tool more useful, I developed the DISC II Temperament Assessment which identifies a person's natural temperament blend. Once I have validated the temperament blend and pattern with the client, I know the following: strengths and weaknesses, natural needs, basic drives, natural fears, method of thinking and reasoning, potential causes of stress and anxiety, typical responses to pressure and stress, potential areas of relationship conflicts, causes of depression, approach to accomplishing a task, causes of procrastination, the traits needed for balance, the keys to relating to them effectively, and more.

Without the temperament information, it would take many interviews to ascertain the same information. Using the temperament model to gain such information facilitates my belief that the counseling process should not be lengthy. My approach to counseling is to help people resolve their presenting issue as quickly as possible so they can get on with their lives.

A benefit of using the temperament model of behavior in counseling is that after validating a client's temperament pattern, the client easily opens up about personal issues. They trust me quickly because they see that I really do understand them.

Another benefit of using the temperament model of behavior in counseling is that the message to clients is that they are normal. Many people go through life comparing themselves to people they admire or envy and believe that they are inferior. It is easy for them to believe that others are normal but they are not.

When the client is able to see themselves in the context of the four temperaments, and identify with others with the same blend, they have a sense of belonging—they are not alone. It is comforting and relieving to find out that there are others that think and feel the same way they do, and that they are exactly the person they were designed and need to be!

Knowing a person's temperament opens up many areas of discussion that may not have otherwise been possible. Clients benefit beyond the reason that brought them to counseling.

DIAGNOSTIC LABELS

When using this model of behavior, I discovered that certain temperaments are associated with certain diagnoses. Furthermore, some diagnoses are exclusive to some temperament blends.

In general, a diagnostic label is the result of one failing to control their natural temperament tendencies. The greater the lack of self-control the greater the possibility one will be tagged with a diagnostic label, which is usually followed by a recommendation to be put on medication to treat the malady. I often tell clients that medication will do for you what you are not willing to do for yourself. I explain that if you exercise self-control, develop coping skills, and become accountable and responsible for what you think, feel, and do, you will be able to handle the circumstances of life and cope more effectively.

When someone comes to me having been given a diagnostic label, I have found that it is often used as an excuse for selfish, inappropriate behavior. For example, people have said, "I did that because I am bipolar." My response to that is: "Not true, you did that because you chose to behave that way." Apart from a drug induced state or brain injury, does behavior just happen without prior thought and decision? Even impulsive behavior is a choice!

As soon as people give up accountability and responsibility for their behavior they are going to live a selfish, self-centered, even self-absorbed life that is full of frustrations. They blame others for their misery and go through life wondering why it did not work for them. They fail to look in the mirror. They do not just burn bridges, they blow them up.

SUMMARY

The field of psychology has largely ignored the temperament model of behavior. A major debate within psychology is which has the greatest influence on a person; nature or nurture. There is no greater natural influence on behavior than a person's temperament, yet it is overlooked in psychology and counseling.

The nature position holds that people are born pre-wired with certain traits and knowledge. This aligns with the temperament model of behavior which holds that people are born with natural tendencies. The nurture position holds that a child's behavioral style is formed as the child responds to their environment.

All agree that what one receives as a child from their primary caregiver is vitally important to how well adjusted they are as they grow and develop into an adult. However, how the individual uses their natural tendencies in their environment is a choice they make regardless of the quality of their environment.

Over 200 years ago, the English poet, William Wordsworth, said "The child is the father of the man." Even he recognized that the choices the child makes, forms the adult. We are all responsible to use and control our natural tendencies and be a productive person in society.

PART II

PRIMARY TEMPERAMENTS & TEMPERAMENT BLENDS

NOTE:

In chapters six through nine you will find repetition when discussing one of the four temperaments. For example, you will notice that the four patterns of the Choleric temperament have similar things said about each one. This is because each blend is made up of 70% of primary temperament and 30% of the second temperament tendencies. In each blend I have identified the influence the second temperament has on each blend. By including the tendencies of the primary temperament along with the tendencies of the second temperament you are able to get the full impact of that blend without reviewing other sections.

<u>CHAPTER</u> **SIX**

THE CHOLERIC | HIGH D
PRIMARY & TEMPERAMENT BLENDS

Cholerics are naturally result-oriented. They have active, positive and forward movement in an antagonistic environment. They influence their environment by overcoming opposition to get results. The Choleric is the least occurring of the four temperaments and a female Choleric is very rare. The Choleric temperament has three combinations and four common patterns:

COMBINATION	PATTERN
Choleric-Sanguine	Executive & Motivator
Choleric-Phlegmatic	Director
Choleric-Melancholy	Strategist

The traits of the primary temperament, Choleric, will be altered or modified in some significant way because of the influence of the secondary temperament. Remember, there are at least three levels of intensity of a temperament: classic, moderate and mild. Some Cholerics will be very strong, others somewhat strong, and still others more mild.

Cholerics are extroverted, hot-tempered, quick-thinking, active, practical, strong-willed, and easily annoyed. They are self-confident, self-sufficient, and very independent minded. They are brief, direct, to the point, and firm when communicating with others. Cholerics like pressure and are easily bored when things are not happening fast enough. They are bold and like to take risks.

Cholerics are domineering, decisive, opinionated, and they find it easy to make decisions for themselves as well as for others. They wake up wanting to control, change or overcome something, anything! They leave little room for negotiating—it's usually their way or no way.

Cholerics are visionaries and seem to never run out of ideas, plans and goals, which are all usually practical. They do not require as much sleep as the other temperaments, so their activity seems endless. Their activity, however, always has a purpose because of their goal-oriented nature.

Cholerics usually do not give in to the pressure of what others think unless they see that they cannot get their desired results. They can be crusaders against social injustice and they love to fight for a cause. They are slow to build relationships, and tend to have only a few close friends, because results are more important than people. Cholerics do not easily empathize with the feelings of others or show compassion. They think big and seek positions of authority.

The philosopher Immanuel Kant (1798), in his book, *Anthropology from a Pragmatic Point of View*, states:

> We say of a choleric man he is fiery, burns up quickly like straw-fire, and can be readily appeased if others give in to him; there is no hatred in his anger, and in fact he loves someone all the more for promptly giving in to him. In short, the choleric is the least fortunate of all the temperaments, since it is the one that arouses most opposition to itself.

The theologian Ole Hallesby (1962) says this about the Choleric in *Temperament and the Christian Fatih*:

> The will is the predominant natural element. It is the will that reacts first to external impressions. What the choleric person experiences leads him at once to some decision and his decisions usually result in action.

A word of caution is necessary. The Choleric temperament is often misunderstood and misapplied to others. Those who know about the four temperaments will say a person is Choleric when they are being assertive or direct. Just because someone acts this way does not mean that they are Choleric by nature. The litmus test is whether or not the Choleric is matter-of-fact, brief, direct, and to the point without being offensive. Others who do these things and do not have the Choleric temperament tend to be abrasive and offensive. This will become more clear as you learn about the behavior of the other temperaments.

The following represents Cholerics in general but individual differences will occur based on the influence of the second temperament. Also, what a person is exposed to from an early age plays a vital role in these areas, but remember an individual is still responsible for the choices they make. Regardless of one's natural tendencies, discipline applied in any area will control and overcome a weakness or extreme behavior. The goal is to become a well-balanced person, being in control of thoughts, feelings, and behavior.

MONEY MANAGEMENT

Cholerics view money as power because of their large ego. Their natural tendency is to spend big and spend often. They naturally think of accomplishing big things so they will not hesitate to spend available resources to accomplish their objective. Cholerics also possess high confidence that they can earn more money.

TIME MANAGEMENT

Cholerics naturally value time because they have a strong sense of urgency to accomplish results quickly. They do not waste time. Cholerics tend to work long hours and expect others to do the same.

DECISION MAKING

Decision making comes easy for Cholerics in part because they are able to see the big picture and how all the parts fit together. They are capable of making decisions quickly based on a relatively small amount of information. They also like to make decisions for others. Cholerics know the results they want so they will not hesitate to make a decision quickly regardless of the consequences—as long as it will produce results.

RELATIONSHIPS

Cholerics tend to not take the time to build relationships that are strictly social. They tend to build relationships that will benefit them professionally or personally. Cholerics are not the affectionate, warm, cozy, "sit by the fire" type.

LEADERSHIP STYLE

Cholerics are naturally controlling, demanding, and directive of those under their leadership. Since they place a high value on results they will not tolerate a lack of a sense of urgency, signs of weakness, hesitation, or failure to obtain results quickly. They push others to achieve more results, faster. Cholerics are rarely satisfied with the status quo. Those under their leadership often experience burnout because of the constant pressure to produce results.

EATING HABITS

Cholerics see eating as a necessary waste of time. They eat because they have to and they will eat while doing something else. They will even eat standing up! Their attitude is that eating just gets in the way of getting more stuff done. Since they possess such a strong ego, they easily restrain themselves from eating too much.

AS A MATE

Cholerics are the least affectionate of the four temperaments. Their mate will never have to wonder what they are thinking--they speak their mind easily, directly, and often. They are quick and confident in decision making and will make decisions for their mate as well.

Cholerics will assume everything is okay in their marriage while they anchor themselves in their work. They typically take the approach, "I told you on our wedding night that I love you, if I change my mind I will let you know!"

These tendencies will be modified depending on the influence of the second temperament and their maturity level. Cholerics, regardless of the blend, have a large ego and it will take a patient, tolerant, understanding mate to have a successful relationship.

THE CHOLERIC | HIGH D BLENDS

THE EXECUTIVE
CHOLERIC-SANGUINE | D-I BLEND

The Choleric-Sanguine blend is expressed in the Executive and Motivator patterns. The Executive pattern has less Sanguine tendencies than the Motivator pattern and is, therefore, more forceful and result-oriented. They actually expect the environment to adapt to their demands. The Motivator pattern is discussed next. The Executive is one of the least frequently found patterns.

The Executive pattern is driven by two temperament needs. The primary need is to get results. The secondary need is to be accepted socially. Either need may dominate their behavior depending on the requirements of the situation. When the Choleric and the Sanguine natural tendencies are combined in the Executive's blend, it produces a result-oriented person who needs to be around people socially some of the time.

DESCRIPTION

Executives have a natural drive to get results, now. The Executive is quickly aroused emotionally but easily calmed. They are goal and bottom-line oriented and can be very persuasive in promoting their ideas. They are easily annoyed when others do not comply with their instructions or direction but it passes quickly. They are not angry, although others may think they are furious. They are impatient and will push others to obtain results and be productive.

They take a win/lose approach to life, so when results are not coming quickly enough they become bored and will move easily to another project. They have boundless energy and need lots of activity. They require little sleep (4 to 6 hours is common). They dislike details or doing tedious work.

Executives need daily challenges and others willing to listen to them and carry out their plans. This versatile, eager, self-starter is very competitive. They like having power and authority and will actively seek leadership positions. They want to be in charge because of confidence in their ability to make decisions and get results. Executives are very practical and will use direct methods to get results but still show some interest and concern for people. Executives are driven by an active will which is apparent in their unyielding determination to accomplish their goals. Executives will fight for their way to accomplish a goal, but they can accept momentary defeat, and tend not to be grudge holders. They dislike weakness in those with whom they are associated.

They need some social involvement but not much. They have a high drive to win, work, and control people and events. They have a firm expression, a penetrating stare, and may appear arrogant.

STRENGTHS

The Executive is naturally result-oriented. They speak with confidence and they are direct when expressing their thoughts and feelings—you never have to wonder what they are thinking! They have a drive to get results quickly and move to another project. They are decisive and have good social skills which they use effectively to influence others to get results. They are self-motivated and tend to be a practical problem solver.

WEAKNESSES

The Executive's effectiveness in relationships and productivity in their career are often hindered because of their impatience and lack of empathy. They are easily annoyed and will try to control and dominate others and events. They can be abrupt, blunt, and explosive. They tend to lack compassion. They are vulnerable to others that can help them get quicker results. They do not seem to realize (or care) that they push people too hard to get results. A long lasting relationship with the Executive is difficult for most.

NEEDS

The Executive will perform at their best and be highly motivated if their natural, basic needs are met, such as: having the possibility of getting results quickly, having the freedom to control their schedule, having the opportunity for advancements, having difficult assignments and personal challenges with activity, and the freedom from details. The Executive needs the results to come quickly or they will get bored and move to another project. They also need someone else to give them information that will help them get results (they prefer not to do the research). They need positions of authority due to their high ego strength.

FEARS

Fear tends to create anger. Fear is a primary emotion and anger is a secondary emotion. The Executive may respond with anger if any of their natural fears are realized (or they perceive they may be), such as: a lack of quick results, loss of influence, or others taking advantage of them.

RESPONSE TO PRESSURE

When under pressure or stress, the Executive will likely become intensely abrasive, impatient, intimidating, and more demanding. They can be abrupt, blunt, and dictatorial.

The Executive will likely release frustration by a sudden outburst of anger or by becoming intensely involved in work or play. Their frustration passes quickly.

CAUSES OF PROCRASTINATION

The Executive will likely procrastinate because they fail to see how doing the activity will help them accomplish their goals or get results quickly. They will sometimes promise too much and forget to follow through. It is not unusual for them to procrastinate because something else gets their attention and is more important.

To avoid procrastination, the Executive needs to decide how the activity will enable them to accomplish their goals and get better, faster results.

TRAITS NEEDED FOR BALANCE

In order to be a more balanced person, the Executive needs to incorporate the following into their behavior: accommodating attitude, consistent effort, organization, more detail planning, empathy, and compassion.

KEYS TO RELATING

To effectively relate to the Executive, be brief, direct, to the point, and show confidence. Stress saving time, be result-oriented, and give them options from which to choose. Remove or reduce the risk of them being taken advantage of, especially in business transactions. Ask "what" questions instead of "how" questions. It's okay to ask questions to gain a better understanding about what they are asking of you.

When responding to their questions do not be wordy, and speed up your responses. If they interrupt you, and they likely will, ask their permission to continue and be non-emotional and matter-of-fact in your responses. Do not withdraw when they get assertive. When in agreement, agree with the facts, not the individual--their ego is already big enough! Be practical and focus on goals, objectives, and ideas.

Be prepared for aggressive responses, even explosive behavior at times. Do not take it personally. When presenting a new idea, be organized, give alternatives, and then ask for their opinion. They may or may not ask for your preference.

Be prepared to give an occasional shock in order to get their attention--they get so focused on a goal that nothing else is important. Be prepared for them to force their ideas on you. Listen patiently and do not react but rather respond without emotion and be matter-of-fact. Always be open and willing to discuss how to get better and faster results.

Never show a lack of confidence and do not waste their time. Never criticize them personally, you may get an explosive response. The Executive will accept criticism of their work if it will facilitate getting better, faster results.

In conversation, the Executive responds best to words and phrases such as: bottom line, save time, quick results, productive, goals, options, and effective. They do not like being asked to repeat something they've said, it will quickly annoy them.

THE MOTIVATOR
CHOLERIC-SANGUINE | D-I BLEND

The Choleric-Sanguine blend is expressed in the Executive and Motivator patterns as previously mentioned. The Motivator pattern is driven by two temperament needs. The primary need is to get results. The secondary need is to be accepted socially. Either need may dominate their behavior depending on the requirements of the situation. When the Choleric and the Sanguine natural tendencies are combined in the Motivator's blend, it produces a result-oriented person who values relationships.

The Motivator pattern has more Sanguine tendencies than the Executive pattern and is, therefore, more charming and inspirational. This is the major difference in these two patterns. The Motivator pattern is one of the least found in society.

DESCRIPTION

Motivators have a natural, strong confidence in their ability to influence people and get results quickly. They have a firm but lively expression. They have a high drive to win, work, and control people and events. They tend to be egotistical, enthusiastic, and very energetic. They like having power and authority. The Motivator is quickly aroused emotionally but easily calmed--especially after others give in to their demands. They can be very charming. They easily and naturally influence and inspire others to take action. They easily convince others to their point of view. They are quickly annoyed when others do not comply to their instruction or direction.

They are usually practical and use direct methods to get results quickly while maintaining relationships with people. They are goal and bottom-line oriented and can be very forceful in promoting their ideas. They tend to be very impatient and will often take a win/lose approach to life.

They want to be in charge because of confidence in their ability to make better decisions. Motivators have boundless energy and need activity and quick results, or they will become bored. This versatile, eager self-starter is very competitive. They need daily, personal challenges and others willing to listen to them to carry out their plans. They dislike a show of weakness in others.

Motivators fight for what they think is the right way to accomplish a goal, but they can accept momentary defeat and tend not to be grudge holders. They need social involvement and use their social contacts to promote themselves.

They may change careers often. If results are not coming quickly they will move to another project. They require little sleep, having only five to six hours is not unusual. They dislike details, doing research, and doing tedious work.

STRENGTHS

The Motivator easily influences and inspires others to take action. They are highly motivated to get results quickly in order to move on to another project. They thrive on social influence and believe that they can motivate others better than anyone else. They are decisive and confident in everything they do.

WEAKNESSES

The Motivator's effectiveness in relationships and productivity in their career is often hindered because of their impatience and explosiveness. They are easily annoyed and can be very abrupt and blunt, alienating others in the process. They often lack follow-through. They are vulnerable to others who can help them get quicker results.

NEEDS

The Motivator will perform at their best and be self-motivated if their natural, basic needs are met such as: the possibility of quick results, having difficult assignments, personal challenges, activity, and freedom from meticulous details. They need personal involvement with others. They need, and will seek, positions of authority and influence due to their high ego strength. It is important to the Motivator that they are involved with a team. They tend to frustrate others because of pushing them to get more results.

FEARS

Fear tends to create anger. Fear is a primary emotion and anger is a secondary emotion. The Motivator may respond with anger if any of their natural fears are realized (or they perceive they may be), such as: not getting results quickly enough, they experience a loss of social influence, or others taking advantage of them.

RESPONSE TO PRESSURE

When under pressure or stress, the Motivator will likely become abrasive, impatient, and emotionally aggressive. They will likely release their frustration by a sudden outburst of anger or intense activity. They can also become very abrupt, blunt, and overbearing but they usually calm down quickly.

CAUSES OF PROCRASTINATION

The Motivator will likely procrastinate because they fail to see how doing the activity will help them accomplish their goals or get quicker results. They also tend to promise too much and forget to follow through.

To avoid procrastination, the Motivator needs to see how the activity will enable them to accomplish their goals and to get better, faster results.

TRAITS NEEDED FOR BALANCE

In order to be a more balanced person, the Motivator needs to incorporate the following into their behavior: organization, follow-through, more detail planning, and emotional control.

KEYS TO RELATING

Remember, the Executive and Motivator patterns are similar. To effectively relate to the Motivator, be brief, direct, and to the point. Be open, firm, and friendly. Show confidence. Do not repeat your point. Stress saving time, be result-oriented, and give them options from which to choose. Remove or reduce the risk of them being taken advantage of, especially in business transactions. Ask "what" questions instead of "how" questions. It's okay to ask questions to gain a better understanding about what they are asking of you.

When responding to their questions, speed up your responses. If they interrupt you, and they likely will, ask their permission to continue, and be non-emotional and matter-of-fact in your responses. Do not withdraw when they get assertive. When in agreement, agree with the facts and ideas, not the individual. Be practical and focus on goals, objectives, and ideas.

Be prepared for aggressive, sometimes charming responses, and explosive behavior at times. Be prepared to give an occasional shock to get their attention. When presenting a new idea, be organized, give alternatives, state your preference, then ask for their opinion. Be practical. Be prepared for them to try and force their ideas.

Listen patiently and do not react but rather respond without emotion and be matter-of-fact. Always be open and willing to discuss how to get better and faster results.

Do not waste their time and do not be wordy. Do not push building a relationship, allow them to move at their pace. Never criticize them personally. The Motivator will accept criticism of their work if it will facilitate getting better, faster results.

In conversation, the Motivator responds best to words and phrases, such as: bottom line, this will save time, quick results, productive, goals, options, team, quick, and effective. Remember, they do not like being asked to repeat anything they have said.

THE DIRECTOR
CHOLERIC-PHLEGMATIC | D-S BLEND

The Choleric-Phlegmatic blend is driven by two temperament needs. Their primary need is to get results. Their secondary need is to accommodate others. Either need may dominate their behavior depending on the requirements of the situation. When the Choleric and the Phlegmatic natural tendencies are combined in the Director's blend it produces a result-oriented person who is unemotional and unyielding when attempting to accomplish a goal.

The Director is more individualistic and unyielding than the other Choleric patterns. The Director is one of the least frequently found patterns.

DESCRIPTION

The Director is naturally a result-oriented, determined, unemotional, and focused individual. The Director has a strong, stubborn will. They are independent and individualistic. They have a firm, stoic expression (flat affect) on their face, and they rarely smile. They are not open, friendly, animated or talkative. They slowly build a few close relationships and will help only those they consider to be their friend.

They are confident and may appear aloof. They want to be in charge because of confidence in their ability to make better decisions. They can be very direct, brief, and blunt when answering questions. They tend to be impatient, especially when instructing others. They dislike weakness in others.

They are very practical and will use direct and persistent methods to get results or promote their ideas. Directors can be very blunt and sarcastic when annoyed. They can be very stubborn and resistant to change due to their ability to focus on accomplishing a task. They exhibit an unyielding determination to follow their routine. They are very focused and can bowl over others when pursuing a goal, without showing much concern.

Directors need to know the big picture and have clear, concrete directions before they can function efficiently. They tend to have difficulty working with others because of their independent nature, bluntness, and lack of natural people skills.

They will lose interest in a project once the challenge is gone or the results are not coming quickly enough. They usually have deep personal goals and may fail to identify with the company's goals. They often resist being a team member unless the team agrees with their method of achieving a goal. They get drowsy when sitting for only a few minutes and they are able to go to sleep quickly.

STRENGTHS

The Director has strong self-determination that drives them to be productive in their career. They are unyielding in pursuit of results. They rarely give up once they decide on a goal. They are practical problem solvers. They are direct and confident in their abilities. They are emotionally stable and consistent in everything they do.

WEAKNESSES

The Director's effectiveness in relationships and productivity in their career is often hindered because of being impersonal, unemotional, and blunt. They often lack empathy and compassion and are too impersonal. They can be too independent and seek personal goals instead of company goals. They are easily annoyed and will show a sudden burst of anger when frustrated but it usually subsides quickly.

They are vulnerable to others that can help them get quicker results. They tend to burn people out by pushing them to get more results quicker. They will often stubbornly resist changing their routine.

NEEDS

The Director will perform at their best and be highly motivated if their natural, basic needs are met, such as: the possibility of quick results, the freedom to work alone, difficult assignments, personal challenges, and the freedom from too many details (they can handle some details). They have a strong need for independence, activity with routine, the opportunity for advancement, and someone else to give them information that will help them get quicker results. They have a strong need to control their own schedule and get results quickly so they can move on to another project. If the results are not coming quickly enough, they lose interest and will look for another project. They need and seek positions of authority due to their high ego strength.

FEARS

Fear tends to create anger. Fear is a primary emotion and anger is a secondary emotion. The Director may respond with anger if any of their natural fears are realized (or they perceive they may be realized), such as: not getting results quickly, expressing emotion, and having too much social involvement. The Director may also respond with anger if it is perceived that they have been taken advantage of, especially in a business transaction.

RESPONSE TO PRESSURE

When under pressure or stress, the Director may become abrasive, sarcastic, and dictatorial. They will likely release their frustration by a sudden burst of anger. They will likely withdraw and rest or sleep excessively.

CAUSES OF PROCRASTINATION

The Director will likely procrastinate because they fail to see how doing the activity will help them accomplish their goals. They may also get bored and lose interest in the project.

To avoid procrastination, the Director needs to see how the activity will enable them to accomplish their goals and get better, faster results.

TRAITS NEEDED FOR BALANCE

In order to be a more balanced person, the Director needs to incorporate the following characteristics into their behavior: openness and friendliness, sensitivity, more empathy and compassion for others, diplomacy, and more personal or social involvement with others.

KEYS TO RELATING

To effectively relate to the Director be non-emotional and matter-of-fact in conversation. Be brief, direct, and to the point, show confidence, and remove or reduce the risk of being taken advantage of, especially in a business transaction. Ask "what" questions instead of "how" questions. Stress saving time and be bottom-line oriented. Give them options from which to choose.

When responding to their questions, slow down your responses. If they interrupt you, and they likely will, ask their permission to continue and be non-emotional and matter-of-fact in your responses. When in agreement, agree with the facts, not the individual. Be practical and focus on goals, objectives, and ideas.

When presenting a new idea, be organized, give alternatives, state your preference, and then ask for their opinion.

Be prepared to give an occasional shock to get their attention. Be prepared for them to push their ideas. Listen patiently and do not react, rather respond without emotion and be matter-of-fact. Always be open and willing to discuss how to get better and faster results.

Never show a lack of confidence and do not be wordy. Never criticize them personally. The Director will accept criticism of their work if it will facilitate getting better, faster results.

In conversation, they like quick, brief answers or they quickly become annoyed. Be prepared for brief, blunt responses, and a lack of emotional expression. Keep the conversation focused on a task, not the relationship.

The Director responds best to words such as practical, effective, bottom line, productive, save time, results, goals, and team. They do not like being asked to repeat something they have said.

THE STRATEGIST
CHOLERIC-MELANCHOLY | D-C BLEND

The Choleric-Melancholy blend is driven by two needs. Their primary need is to get results. The secondary need is to do things right. Either need may dominate their behavior depending on the requirements of the situation. When the Choleric and the Melancholy tendencies are combined in the Strategist's blend, it produces a result-oriented, detailed person who plans and pushes their way through life. The Strategist will always operate from a well-thought through, detailed plan.

Strategists are more detail oriented and sensitive than the other Choleric blends. The Strategist is a frequently found pattern.

DESCRIPTION

The Strategist is a result-oriented, detailed person who is not interested in social involvement. They are driven by a strong will to achieve their detailed plan. They can be direct, blunt, and forceful, yet at times show great sensitivity. They can be both domineering and compassionate (they can be both a Lion and a Lamb). They are easily annoyed and quickly aroused, but easily calmed down.

They are a creative problem solver who naturally develops strategies to achieve a goal. They function best when they collect facts and have alone time to think and develop a plan of action. In the process of developing their plan, they will ask direct and detailed questions and can be very forceful and blunt. They prefer work to involvement with people. They have confidence in their voice.

Children are easily drawn to them because of their confidence and sensitive side. Children feel secure in their presence. They initiate change and operate from a well-thought-out plan and have creative, problem-solving skills. Strategists will often use very direct, forceful, and persistent methods to get results or promote their ideas. They want to be in charge because of the confidence in their ability to make things happen the right way. Strategists like to solve problems and make decisions and are actually quite capable of doing so. They usually have clear goals and are very independent in their attempt to carry them out. They need to know exactly what is expected before they can function efficiently.

They speak with authority and are usually very productive in whatever they undertake. When committed to accomplishing a goal they are insightful and creative. They dislike weakness in others and do not like to repeat what they have said.

STRENGTHS

The Strategist is creative, practical, and will operate from a detailed plan in order to get results. They are creative, direct, and decisive. They respond well to a challenge by developing a detailed strategy to accomplish the objective. Actually, they are excellent at developing strategies to solve problems and will get excited about having a problem to analyze and solve. Once the plan is determined, they are very confident in their ability to obtain the desired results. They seek difficult tasks. If they are not involved in a challenging task, they become bored and restless.

WEAKNESSES

The Strategist's effectiveness in relationships and productivity in their career is often hindered because of their impatience and lack of sensitivity, compassion, and empathy. They can be explosive when frustrated by a lack of results. They tend to do crisis communication. They can be moody which is caused by thinking too much about the wrong thing. They are vulnerable to others who can help them get quicker results. People under them experience burnout because of being pushed to get quicker results. They often have difficulty delegating responsibility because they want to maintain too much control. They have difficulty trusting others.

NEEDS

The Strategist will perform at their best and be highly motivated if their basic, natural needs are met, such as the possibility of quick results, freedom to establish their own schedule, information that will help them get quick results, and the chance to make something better. They need difficult assignments that require detailed planning. They need activity, challenges, independence, positions of authority, and the opportunity for advancement. They need others to carry out their plans. They need, and will seek, positions of authority due to their large ego strength.

FEARS

Fear tends to create anger. Fear is a primary emotion and anger is a secondary emotion. The Strategist may respond with anger if any of their natural fears are realized (or they perceive they may be realized) such as others taking advantage of them, a lack of quick results, or loss of control, or too much social involvement.

RESPONSE TO PRESSURE

When under pressure or stress, the Strategist can become abrasive, blunt, critical, and moody. They can also become impatient and dictatorial. They release their frustration by a sudden burst of anger or they become intensely involved in their work. They often withdraw to think, review, and plan to solve a problem.

CAUSES OF PROCRASTINATION

The Strategist will likely procrastinate because they fail to see how doing the activity will help them accomplish their goals. They may also fail to see the reason why it should be done.

Frustration occurs, which may lead to procrastination, when the secondary need to think and plan interferes with the primary need for results. These two drives often clash with each other resulting in a lack of decisiveness and action. This is caused by a lack of having sufficient information which interferes with formulating a plan of action or strategy. Once they have gathered enough information and a plan is determined, the Strategist can function with precision.

TRAITS NEEDED FOR BALANCE

In order to be a more balanced person, the Strategist needs to be more sensitive and compassionate toward others and exercise more emotional control. They also need to be more socially involved. They need to have more consistency.

KEYS TO RELATING

To effectively relate to the Strategist, be brief, direct, and to the point. Show confidence. Give detailed options and remove the risk of being taken advantage of, especially in a business transaction. Be result-oriented and stress saving time. Be practical. Do not be wordy and get to the point quickly.

The Strategist responds best to words such as results, plan, detail, bottom line, goals, practical, save time, quick, and effective.

In conversation, if they interrupt you, and they probably will, ask their permission to continue, and then be matter-of-fact in your responses. They like quick, short answers or they will become annoyed. Be prepared for brief, blunt responses. Keep the conversation focused on the task, not the relationship. They do not like being asked to repeat anything they've said.

When presenting a new idea, be organized, give alternatives, state your preference, and then ask for their opinion. Ask "what" questions instead of "how" questions. Stress saving time and be bottom-line oriented. When in agreement, agree with the facts, not the individual. Be practical and focus on goals, objectives, and ideas.

Be prepared to give an occasional shock to get their attention. Be prepared for them to push their ideas forcefully. Listen patiently and do not react, rather respond without emotion, and be matter-of-fact. Always be open and willing to discuss how to get better and faster results.

Never show a lack of confidence and never criticize them personally. Their high sense of self will usually not accept personal criticism without a negative, sometimes aggressive response. The Strategist will, however, accept criticism of their work if it will facilitate getting better, faster results.

CHAPTER **SEVEN**

THE SANGUINE | HIGH I
PRIMARY & TEMPERAMENT BLENDS

Sanguines are naturally people-oriented. They have an active, positive movement in a favorable environment. They influence their environment by encouraging others to work together. The Sanguine temperament has three combinations and four common patterns that frequently appear:

COMBINATION	PATTERN
Sanguine-Choleric	Negotiator-Marketer
Sanguine-Phlegmatic	Relater
Sanguine-Melancholy	Performer

The traits of the primary temperament, Sanguine, will be altered or modified in some significant way due to the influence of the secondary temperament. Remember, there are at least three levels of intensity of a temperament: classic, moderate, and mild. Some Sanguines will be very strong, others somewhat strong, and still others more mild. Some are "super Sanguines" because they are so talkative and active that they are overwhelming.

Sanguines are extroverted, fun-loving, playful, activity-prone, impulsive, entertaining, persuasive, easily amused and optimistic. They are enthusiastic, expressive and tend to be very affectionate. Sanguines are personable, receptive, open to others, and build relationships quickly. They are animated, excitable, approachable, accepting and trusting of others. They will smile and talk easily and often. Sanguines are word smiths.

It is not unusual to feel as if you have known one who is Sanguine for years after the first meeting. They make and keep friends easily. They get so involved in conversations that they easily forget about time and are often late arriving at their destination. Sanguines are easily bored if not involved in social activity. Sanguines dislike solitude. Their attention span is based on whether or not they are interested in the person or event. They can change their focus or interest in an instant if they become bored.

When telling a story, Sanguines often exaggerate what happened or leave out important details. They make the story exciting and they don't let the facts get in the way!

Sanguines are competitive and tend to be disorganized. They sometimes have difficulty controlling their thoughts and emotions. Actually, they tend not to store their thoughts and feelings—if they think it or feel it, they share it! They usually like sports of any kind because of the activity and involvement with people. Their voice will show excitement and friendliness. Sanguines enjoy dressing according to current fashion. They fear rejection or not making a favorable impression. Sanguines also fear others viewing them as unsuccessful. Sanguines are very effective working with others.

The philosopher, Immanuel Kant (1798), in his book, *Anthropology from a Pragmatic Point of View*, says:

A sanguine person manifests his way of sensing and can be recognized by the following traits: he is carefree and full of hope; he attaches great importance to each thing for the moment, and the next moment may not give it another thought. He makes promises in all honesty, but fails to keep his word because he has not reflected deeply enough beforehand whether he will be able to keep it. He is a good companion and high-spirited, who is reluctant to take anything seriously and all men are his friends.

The theologian Ole Hallesby (1962) says this about the Sanguine in *Temperament and the Christian Faith*:

The sanguine attitude toward one's surroundings is a receptive mood. Impressions from without have easy access to mind and heart. The explanation for this receptivity of spirit lies in the fact that in the sanguine temperament, the feelings are predominant. And it is one's feelings that are most easily stirred by impressions from without.

The following represents Sanguines in general but individual differences will occur based on the influence of the second temperament. Also, what a person is exposed to from an early age plays a vital role in these areas, but remember an individual is still responsible for the choices they make. Regardless of one's natural tendencies, discipline applied in any area will control and overcome a weakness or extreme behavior. The goal is to become a well-balanced person, being in control of thoughts, feelings, and behavior.

MONEY MANAGEMENT

Sanguines view money as giving them the freedom to enjoy life. Their natural tendency is to spend often on play things, status things or on things they just want. Sanguines' biggest enemy is instant gratification. They see it, they want it, and they feel good when they buy it--not having the money is never a deterrent as long as they have room on one of their credit cards! Credit card companies and debt counselors love Sanguines!

DECISION MAKING

Sanguines frequently make impulsive decisions. Not much thought will precede the quick decision and consequences are considered later. They often take the approach of "ready, fire, aim!" Sanguines will often express remorse for a poor decision but soon forget the unwanted consequences and repeat the behavior. Sanguines tend to have difficulty making an objective decision because they are too concerned about how their decision will make them look in front of others.

RELATIONSHIPS

Sanguines naturally build relationships that are social. They make friends easily and often and enjoy being around people and having fun. They know the largest number of people and will usually have a wide network of friends, both personal and professional. This is why Facebook is so popular! Sanguines are the affectionate, warm, cozy, "sit by the fire" type.

LEADERSHIP STYLE

Sanguines are naturally friendly and open to those under their leadership. They will likely want everyone to be their friend. They usually take a team approach to management wanting everyone to cooperate. Sanguines are easy to follow because they naturally communicate acceptance to others. They often have difficulty when they need to confront someone.

EATING HABITS

Sanguines tend to view food as a celebration. They enjoy the event of eating with others--life is a party to Sanguines. Once the party gets started, they exercise little restraint and will likely overeat. Of course, some Sanguines will control their eating habits driven by their need to have an acceptable appearance in the eyes of others.

AS A MATE

Sanguines are the most affectionate of the four temperaments. They require a lot of touch, affection, and interaction from their mate. Sanguines are flexible, spontaneous, impulsive, and talkative--this requires a lot of patience from their mate.

Sanguines have a natural smile and they like to be on the go or with people most of the time. Do not expect them to just sit and watch the world go by--they are not spectators, they are participants in life. Sanguines like sports and outside activities. They are so people-oriented that they often forget about time when they are enjoying themselves--this of course, can cause tension with their mate because of not being where they are supposed to be, on time. They tend to do things to excess.

Sanguines can be very romantic and they enjoy celebrating just about anything. Sanguines are usually so fun-oriented that it takes a patient, tolerant, understanding mate to be in a successful relationship with them.

These tendencies will be modified depending on the influence of the second temperament and their maturity level.

THE SANGUINE | HIGH I BLENDS

THE NEGOTIATOR
SANGUINE-CHOLERIC | I-D BLEND

The Sanguine-Choleric blend is expressed in the Negotiator and Marketer patterns. The Sanguine-Choleric is driven by two temperament needs. The primary need is to be accepted socially. The secondary need is to get results. Either need may dominate their behavior depending on the requirements of the situation.

When the Sanguine and the Choleric natural tendencies are combined in the Negotiator's blend, it produces a people-person who is goal-oriented, and pushes their way through life trying to persuade others to their point of view.

The Negotiator pattern has more Choleric tendencies and is, therefore, more forceful and result oriented than the Marketer pattern, which is discussed next. The Negotiator is a somewhat common pattern.

DESCRIPTION

Negotiators are more assertive than the other Sanguine blends and they easily convince others to their point of view. Negotiators are very persuasive and make good debaters! They are very energetic and work well with and through people and make good leaders. They have an outgoing interest in others and the ability to gain the respect and confidence of various types of individuals. They strive to do business in a friendly way while pushing forward to win their objectives. They have a firm, lively, and friendly expression.

They are able to coordinate events and willing to delegate responsibilities. They exhibit poise and confidence in most situations, especially social events. They will become bored without activity and social involvement.

Negotiators have a difficult time with details, organization, and consistency. They prefer that others give them information that will help them make decisions rather than research it for themselves. They are very optimistic but may lack follow through.

The Negotiator has a high need to be with, around, or close to people. They will be active or with people all the time. The Negotiator, however, tends to know lots of people but they do not know lots of people well--they do not take the time to do so. They are naturally positive, energetic, and enthusiastic about life. They are easily excited and they have a winsome expression. They are able to persuade others to their point of view without being offensive. However, they can be egotistical and overbearing at times. They like to tell others what to do and can be too pushy. They live in the present and they dislike details and structure. They do not plan and will likely "make it up when they wake up!" They often display an attitude that everything they have or do is better. They are competitive. They work in spurts because they like to play. Also, they do not like doing the same thing for very long before they look for something to break the monotony of the moment.

STRENGTHS

The Negotiator temperament has a strong, natural ability to persuade and influence others to their point of view. For this reason they are regarded as the most powerful of all the temperament blends. They are excellent debaters, salespeople, and natural negotiators. They are friendly, open, sociable, and have contagious enthusiasm. They like a challenge and starting new projects. They are natural leaders--people easily follow them.

WEAKNESSES

The Negotiator's effectiveness in relationships and productivity in their career is often hindered because of a lack of organization and planning, impulsiveness, and they often lack follow-through. They tend to play and talk too much. They can become verbally forceful when communicating their views. They overuse telling others what to do.

NEEDS

The Negotiator will perform at their best and will be highly motivated if their natural, basic needs are met, such as: contact with people, acceptance from others, activity, and the opportunity to build social relationships. They have a strong need to be recognized for their accomplishments (this is important to their sense of well-being). They need the freedom to express themselves, to be active, and to have the opportunity to persuade others.

FEARS

Fear tends to create anger. Fear is a primary emotion and anger is a secondary emotion. The Negotiator may respond with anger if any of their natural fears are realized (or they perceive they may be realized), such as being rejected or embarrassed, losing, not being able to influence others, not having the freedom to be active, or they are asked to do detailed work.

RESPONSE TO PRESSURE

When under pressure or stress, the Negotiator will likely become restless, rebel, and talk extensively about the issue. They may deny the reality of the situation and manipulate others by trying to persuade them with strong emotion to their point of view. They may not listen to another position, believing their position is better. They often release their frustration by being verbally aggressive.

CAUSES OF PROCRASTINATION

Negotiators will likely procrastinate because they fear rejection or they do not remember what they promised to do. They do mean well but they often take on more than they can do.

The Negotiator can increase their effectiveness by writing down what needs to be done, reviewing the list during the day and deciding to take action.

TRAITS NEEDED FOR BALANCE

In order to be a more balanced person, the Negotiator needs to incorporate the following into their behavior: organization, patience, consistency, follow-through, detailed planning, structure, and routine.

KEYS TO RELATING

To effectively relate to the Negotiator, remember they can be both assertive and fun-loving. So, show excitement, have fun, smile, and be prepared for them to try to persuade you to their point of view with emotion. It is very important to remove the risk of looking bad or the possibility of being embarrassed. They want to be your friend.

In conversation, the Negotiator responds best to words, such as exciting, latest, status, together, fun, and team.

SANGUINE-CHOLERIC | I-D BURNOUT

The Sanguine-Choleric is the only blend that has a tendency to burnout frequently. Both patterns, Negotiator and Marketer, are affected by this reoccurring event. Typical symptoms of burnout include three to five weeks of excessive activity expending intense energy, followed by one to three days of low energy with little or no activity and the need for isolation and rest. The Negotiator uses lots of energy and once their energy level is depleted, rest and down time follows, which allows their body to restore the energy that was used.

To control the effects and reduce the frequency of burnout, the Negotiator should consider reducing their intensity level and taking several five-minute pauses during the day to relax. There are other relaxation techniques that can be practiced daily--do a little research.

The intensity level can also be reduced and you will, therefore, become more productive. Establish a schedule or routine before the day begins, become more organized, and have a variety of activities instead of one single focus.

THE MARKETER
SANGUINE-CHOLERIC | I-D BLEND

The Sanguine-Choleric blend is expressed in the Marketer and Negotiator patterns. The Sanguine-Choleric is driven by two temperament needs. The primary need is to be accepted socially. The secondary need is to get results. Either need may dominate their behavior depending on the requirements of the situation.

When the Sanguine and the Choleric natural tendencies are combined in the Marketer's blend, it produces a people-person who easily excites others. They have a lively expression and they will smile easily and laugh often.

The Marketer pattern has less Choleric tendencies and is, therefore, more excitable than the Negotiator pattern. The Marketer is a somewhat common pattern.

DESCRIPTION

The Marketer wants to be with people or be active most of the time. They rarely like being alone or inactivity. They are, by far, the most enthusiastic of the other Sanguine blends. They can get very excited. These are assertive and energetic people who work well with and through others. They have an outgoing interest in others and they have the ability to gain the respect and confidence of various types of individuals. They strive to do business in a friendly way while pushing forward to win their objectives. They easily promote their own ideas or the ideas of others. They exhibit poise and confidence in most situations, especially social events. Marketers become bored without activity and social involvement.

They have difficulty with awareness of time, organizing, and concentrating on details. They prefer others to give them information that will help them make decisions rather than research it for themselves. They are very optimistic and enthusiastic but lack consistent follow-through. At times, they can display a superior attitude that everything they have and do is better.

The Marketer, like the Negotiator, tends to know lots of people but they do not know lots of people well--they do not take the time to do so. They get excited about most everything. They have a lively, friendly, open expression, and will talk a lot.

Their intensity and acceptance of people naturally elevates the emotional level of others. They can raise the level of emotion just entering a room full of people. They are very active socially and they like to drop names of people they know.

They have a strong dislike for details and structure but a stronger dislike for routine. They are a "now" person and work in spurts because of their difficulty concentrating on accomplishing one thing at a time. They are easily distracted, disorganized, and tend to be inconsistent. They experience emotional burnout often (more later at the end of this section). Like the Negotiator pattern, they too will likely "make it up when they wake up!"

STRENGTHS

The Marketer has a natural ability to stir excitement in others. They are full of optimism and enthusiasm. Their contagious emotion naturally lifts the spirits of others just by being in their presence. They are open, sociable, and friendly. They naturally develop a large network of people both personally and professionally.

WEAKNESSES

The Marketer's effectiveness in relationships and productivity in their career is often hindered because of a lack of organization and planning. They tend to be inconsistent and lack follow through. They are impulsive and have a tendency to talk and play too much. They find it difficult to concentrate on doing one thing to completion because they are easily distracted. Their attention span is short. They will overstate and over-promise what they are going to do. They can easily overlook obvious flaws in others because they are so optimistic about people and life in general.

NEEDS

The Marketer will perform at their best and will be highly motivated if their natural, basic needs are met, such as having the freedom to express themselves, a flexible schedule, mobility, involvement with people, recognition, acceptance, freedom from details, contact with people, and an open environment that allows them the opportunity to build a social network.

They need public recognition for their accomplishments, which is important for their sense of well-being. They need someone else to do the details. They need a variety of activities or they will quickly become bored.

FEARS

Fear tends to create anger. Fear is a primary emotion and anger is a secondary emotion. The Marketer may respond with anger if any of their natural fears are realized (or they perceive they may be realized), such as being rejected, being in a fixed environment, details, losing, and not influencing others.

RESPONSE TO PRESSURE

When under pressure or stress, the Marketer will likely become restless, rebellious, and try to manipulate others with emotion. They can deny reality. They need to talk extensively about whatever is bothering them. They often release frustration by becoming verbally aggressive.

CAUSES OF PROCRASTINATION

Marketers may procrastinate to avoid the possibility of being rejected. They may not remember what they promised to do because of their short attention span. Sometimes, they take on more than they can do.

The Marketer can increase effectiveness by writing down what needs to be done, reviewing the list during the day and deciding to take action.

TRAITS NEEDED FOR BALANCE

In order to be a more balanced person, the Marketer needs to incorporate the following into their behavior: organization, follow-through, patience, consistency, structure, and routine.

KEYS TO RELATING

To effectively relate to the Marketer, be lighthearted, have fun, and show excitement. Be prepared to listen and laugh. Remove the risk of being rejected, looking bad, or being embarrassed.

In conversation, the Marketer responds best to words such as: exciting, latest, status, fun, team, and network.

SANGUINE-CHOLERIC | I-D BURNOUT

The Sanguine-Choleric is the only blend that has a tendency to burnout frequently. Both patterns, Negotiator and Marketer, are affected by this reoccurring event. Typical symptoms of burnout include three to five weeks of excessive activity expending intense energy, followed by one to three days of low energy with little or no activity and the need for isolation and rest. The Marketer uses lots of energy and once their energy level is depleted, rest and down time follows, which allows their body to restore the energy that was used.

To control the effects and reduce the frequency of burnout, the Marketer should consider reducing their intensity level and taking several five-minute pauses during the day to relax. There are other relaxation techniques that can be practiced daily--do a little research.

The intensity level can also be reduced and you will, therefore, become more productive. Establish a schedule or routine before the day begins, become more organized, and have a variety of activities instead of one single focus.

THE RELATER
SANGUINE-PHLEGMATIC | I-S BLEND

The Sanguine-Phlegmatic is driven by two temperament needs. The primary need is to be accepted socially. The secondary need is to accommodate others. Either need may dominate their behavior depending on the requirements of the situation.

When the Sanguine and the Phlegmatic natural tendencies are combined in the Relater's blend, it produces a people-person who is accommodating to the needs of others.

Relaters are more relationship oriented and consistent than the other Sanguine blends. The Relater is a frequently found pattern.

DESCRIPTION

The Relater needs to be with people most of the time but some of the time they need to be alone. When alone they will likely rest or sleep. They often become drowsy when sitting still after only a few minutes. They are independent minded and can be very stubborn. Once they establish a routine it is difficult for them to change. They are very trusting of others and place importance on enduring relationships. It is not unusual for them to keep relationships they formed in kindergarten throughout their life-span. They are loyal to their friends. They are optimistic and full of hope. Most Relaters smile easily and often.

Relaters have a calming, friendly, accepting expression. They are disarming with their warm, empathic, and understanding approach. Relaters possess a casual kind of poise in social situations. People tend to seek them out, even strangers, to share their problems because they perceive them to be good listeners. Children are easily drawn to them because they feel accepted in their presence. Although doing details and organizational things give them difficulty at times, they are able to do them quite well. They can be great administrators. Relaters work very well with others because they are optimistic, accepting, and accommodating.

STRENGTHS

The Relater naturally and easily forms lasting relationships. They are accepting of others and project a warm, gentle friendliness. They are understanding, and compassionate with others.

They are the most consistent of the Sanguine blends. Once they establish a routine they tend to follow it with unyielding determination.

WEAKNESSES

The Relater's effectiveness in relationships and productivity in their career is often hindered because of their reluctance to confront others, their disorganization, and impulsiveness. They may play or talk too much. Relaters can be inattentive to details. They may act impulsively without considering the consequences. They can be overly enthusiastic and oversell their ideas.

They can be too optimistic regarding the potential of others. They may overlook obvious flaws in others. The Relater has the natural ability to win friends easily. They naturally project the message that, "I want to be your friend." Sometimes they prefer not to be friends but they do not know how to avoid the relationship without hurting the person's feelings. This can create a dilemma for the Relater.

NEEDS

The Relater will perform at their best and will be highly motivated if their natural, basic needs are met, such as: personal involvement with others, the opportunity to form lasting relationships, and be recognized for their accomplishments.

They need freedom of expression, to be of service to others, activity, and someone else to do the details. They need a routine but with some flexibility and social activity.

FEARS

Fear tends to create anger. Fear is a primary emotion and anger is a secondary emotion. The Relater may respond with anger if any of their natural fears are realized (or they perceive they may be realized), such as: the potential loss of a relationship, living in an unstable environment, criticism, disunity, losing, or being embarrassed, especially in public.

RESPONSE TO PRESSURE

When under pressure or stress, the Relater may deny reality, resist change (become very stubborn) and rebel against authority. They may try to manipulate others with emotion. Since the Relater has a natural fear of confronting or putting pressure on others they may be tempted to misrepresent the reality of the situation in order to avoid the conflict.

The Relater naturally releases their frustration by talking and/or sleeping excessively.

CAUSES OF PROCRASTINATION

Relaters will likely procrastinate when it becomes necessary to confront or put pressure on someone. They may also procrastinate when they are not able to accommodate all concerned or they have to change their routine. They may also forget what they promised to do.

The Relater can increase effectiveness by writing down what needs to be done, reviewing the list during the day and deciding to take action.

It is important for the Relater to understand that when a habit is formed, it forms you. So, form good habits and they will serve you well.

Consider that sometimes confronting someone is often the loving thing to do. Do not think only of yourself and the pain you may feel. Confronting someone may be in their best interest.

TRAITS NEEDED FOR BALANCE

In order to be a more balanced person, the Relater needs to incorporate the following into their behavior: more directness, willingness to state their opinion, willingness to confront others, organization, and more detailed planning.

KEYS TO RELATING

To effectively relate to the Relater, demonstrate warm, friendly acceptance. Stress the importance of lasting relationships. Show excitement and have fun. Remove the risk of being embarrassed. Do not suddenly disrupt their routine. Do not show too much emotion, and do not be too detailed, or picky about little things.

In conversation, the Relater responds best to words such as: relationship, friendship, exciting, fun, loyal, and routine.

THE PERFORMER
SANGUINE-MELANCHOLY | I-C BLEND

The Sanguine-Melancholy is driven by two temperament needs. The primary need is to be accepted socially. The secondary need is to do things right. Either need may dominate their behavior depending on the requirements of the situation.

When the Sanguine and the Melancholy natural tendencies are combined in the Performer's blend, it produces a people-person who is sensitive, creative, and detail-oriented. Performers are more formal and sensitive than the other Sanguine blends. The Performer is a frequently found pattern.

DESCRIPTION

Performers need to be with people most of the time but some of the time they need to be alone. When alone they will likely think, review, plan, and be creative. They need information, time to think, and a plan before they can function effectively. They function best when they have a detailed plan. Once they have a plan, however, they may not be consistent or follow through because of a fear of failure.

Performers have a very active, vivid imagination causing them to be creative in many areas like music, the performing arts, writing, decoration, etc. They tend to be very image conscious and actively seek recognition for their achievements. Performers have a deep need to know that they will be accepted by others. They struggle with guilt feelings. They are usually well organized. Being organized does not necessarily mean that everything is neatly in place. Being organized can also mean that you know where everything is located--if you know what's in the piles then you're organized!

Information about their job is very important to them, so they may ask many questions before accepting a task. They tend to be cautious because they have a deep need to make a favorable impression. They like status and quality things.

They have difficulty going to sleep because they are thinking too much--reviewing, planning, fretting, or creating. The Performer's emotions will likely fluctuate widely, especially if they are embarrassed or they have been, or may be, rejected. They can do many things to an extreme.

Performers tend to warm up slowly to new people because they are unsure of how they are being received. Once they feel safe or accepted, they become more friendly.

STRENGTHS

The Performer has a natural ability to function well socially (once the fear of rejection has been removed) and privately. They need to be with people but they also need to spend time alone. Their alone time allows their creativity to be expressed and developed. They process information quickly.

They have the ability to excel in any artistic field. They have a high drive to win. They persuade others with facts and emotion. They are driven to do a task correctly and make a good impression in the process. They are capable of being the best in their chosen field.

WEAKNESSES

The Performer's effectiveness in relationships and productivity in their career is often hindered because of giving into a variety of fears, such as; the fear of being rejected, the fear of losing, and the fear of being embarrassed or put down.

They often react with extreme emotion if a fear is realized or they perceive something may happen that will be embarrassing. They may demonstrate intense emotion, become critical and condescending, and will want to remove themselves from the situation. They also tend to have emotional highs and lows fueled by critical thinking, being impractical, having high standards, and failure to spend sufficient time alone.

The Performer, may at times, demonstrate an extreme emotional response and get verbally (sometimes physically) aggressive in response to rejection. This is often followed by remorse and lengthy periods of isolation.

NEEDS

The Performer will be at their best and will be highly motivated if their natural, basic needs are met, such as: being with people, feeling accepted, and spending time alone to think, review, plan, and be creative. The amount of daily alone time needed varies with the individual--all need some time alone but some will need more than others. They need a variety of activities and public recognition for their accomplishments.

FEARS

Fear tends to create anger. Fear is a primary emotion and anger is a secondary emotion. The Performer may respond with extreme emotion if any of their natural fears are realized, such as: being rejected, being embarrassed, losing, not doing the task correctly, not making a favorable impression, or being criticized personally.

Performers tend to be reluctant to start a new project until they have confidence that they will not fail. If they cannot be sure that they will succeed, they often do not try. Performers tend to ask lots of specific questions to avoid failure or being embarrassed.

RESPONSE TO PRESSURE

When under pressure or stress, the Performer may react with strong emotion and become angry and critical. They may release their frustration by talking, withdrawing, attacking verbally, or becoming depressed. They may deny the reality of the situation and try to manipulate others to their point of view with intense emotion.

CAUSES OF PROCRASTINATION

Performers will likely procrastinate if they think they may not make a favorable impression or if the risk of failure is too great. They may be unsure of the right way to accomplish the task without failing. They may also forget to do what they promised.

The Performer needs to develop coping skills to handle rejection, failure, and embarrassment. When these things occur, they must learn to not take it personally and decide to learn from the experience and move on.

TRAITS NEEDED FOR BALANCE

In order to be a more balanced person, the Performer needs to incorporate the following into their behavior: control of their fears and emotions, relaxation, consistency, realistic standards, and clear, practical goals. Coping skills are needed to deal with the fear of being rejected.

One of the most important things a Performer can do is to spend sufficient time alone, each day. How much time is relative to the individual. When the Performer does not have sufficient alone time they find it difficult to function effectively.

They need a well thought out plan (not necessarily written down). Family and friends need to understand that it is not selfish for the Performer to spend time alone, it is in their best interest. Of course balance is the key, too much alone time is not healthy.

KEYS TO RELATING

To effectively relate to the Performer, show acceptance and respect. Be somewhat formal until they relax. Remove the risk of them being rejected or embarrassed. Show some excitement and be logical and factual in communication. Have some fun, laugh and smile.

In conversation, the Performer responds best to words, such as: proud, exciting, latest, status, fun, prestigious, think, and plan.

CHAPTER EIGHT

THE PHLEGMATIC | HIGH S
PRIMARY & TEMPERAMENT BLENDS

Phlegmatics are naturally accommodating and service-oriented. They are passive in both favorable and unfavorable environments. They influence their environment by cooperating with others to carry out the task. The Phlegmatic temperament has three combinations and three patterns:

COMBINATION	PATTERN
Phlegmatic-Choleric	Inspector
Phlegmatic-Sanguine	Harmonizer
Phlegmatic-Melancholy	Helper

The traits of the primary temperament, Phlegmatic, will be altered or modified in some significant way determined by the influence of the secondary temperament. Remember, there are at least three levels of intensity of a temperament: classic, moderate, and mild. Some Phlegmatics will be very strong, others somewhat strong, and still others more mild.

Phlegmatics are introverted, calm, unemotional, easygoing, indecisive, patient, and agreeable. They are both slow and indirect when responding to others. Phlegmatics are slow to warm-up but will be accommodating in the process. They are by far the easiest people with whom to get along--as long as you do not try to alter their routine or ask them to change.

Phlegmatics live a quiet, routine life free of the normal anxieties of the other temperaments. They avoid getting too involved with people and life in general preferring a private, low-key life-style centered around home and family.

Phlegmatics seldom exert themselves with others or push their way along in their career. They just let it happen. They make good team players. They communicate a warm, sincere interest in others, preferring to have just a few close friends. They are possessive of their friendships and material things. Phlegmatics will be very loyal to their friends and find it difficult to break long-standing relationships regardless of what the other person does or doesn't do. A mother who has the Phlegmatic temperament will often refer to her children as, "my children," leaving a bewildered look on her husband's face.

Phlegmatics will strongly resist sudden change. They need time to adjust when change does occur, especially sudden change. They tend to avoid conflict and will resist making quick decisions. Phlegmatics are practical, concrete, and traditional thinkers. Their stoic expression often hides their true feelings. They can be grudge holders. Phlegmatics can also be patient to the point of paralysis. They are persistent and consistent at whatever they undertake. Because of their passive nature, they tend to procrastinate easily and often.

The theologian Ole Hallesby (1962) in *Temperament and the Christian Fatih,* says this about the Phlegmatic:

> The phlegmatic has the calm, well-balanced temperament. In the first place, impressions from his surroundings have a far more harmonious effect on the phlegmatic individual than they have on the other temperaments. There is no one side of his nature that is especially active.

The following represents Phlegmatics in general but individual differences will occur. What a person is exposed to from an early age plays a vital role in these areas but remember an individual is still responsible for the choices they make. Regardless of one's natural tendencies, discipline applied in any area will control and overcome weaknesses or extreme behavior. The goal is to become a well-balanced person, being in control of thoughts, feelings, and behavior.

MONEY MANAGEMENT

Phlegmatics view money as security because of their natural tendency to worry excessively. They are reluctant to spend their money because they do not have a need for the latest anything or to replace what they bought years before. When they buy furniture for their home it could sit there for twenty years (or more) and never be moved--they tend to keep the house, car, boat, lamp, coat, pen, mate, etc., forever! Phlegmatics quietly hoard their money and can be financially secure to everyone's surprise.

TIME MANAGEMENT

Phlegmatics tend to be a poor manager of time. They lack a sense of urgency so they will often put off doing a task. They so want to accommodate everyone that it will paralyze them from getting something done in a timely manner. However, if they establish a routine of being on time early in life, they will follow it consistently. Since Phlegmatics tend to not be in a hurry, they experience less stress and therefore live the longest of the four temperaments.

DECISION MAKING

Phlegmatics take an excessive amount of time to make a decision--sometimes they never make the decision! They are paralyzed by their need to accommodate others and they fear their decision with not be met with approval by all involved. So, they put it off until forced to decide--even then it still may not happen.

RELATIONSHIPS

Phlegmatics build a limited number of relationships slowly and will usually never let go regardless of what the individual says or does. They do not have a wide social network preferring to have a few close friends and, of course, their family. Once they become your friend they will be loyal, dependable, and faithful. These are great friends to have because they are dependable. Phlegmatics take awhile to warm up to be the affectionate, warm, cozy, "sit by the fire" type. They respond well to a low-key, peaceful relationship.

LEADERSHIP STYLE

Phlegmatics manage in a low-key, non-emotional manner. They will be soft and accommodating adhering to the established rules and regulations of their environment. Because they do not have a sense of urgency, decisions usually take an excessive amount of time. Because of this, productivity may slow down in their area of responsibility. Phlegmatics will want everyone to be accommodated. This results in stubbornly adhering to "the way we have always done it." Phlegmatics usually take a team approach to management, wanting everyone to cooperate.

They will have difficulty when they need to confront someone because of their fear of conflict and tension.

FOOD

Phlegmatics view food as pleasure. They enjoy eating and will exercise the least restraint of the four temperaments. It is this group that tends to be the most overweight. Their lack of self-discipline encourages poor eating habits--once they start eating it is difficult for them to stop.

AS A MATE

Phlegmatics can be affectionate, but it takes some time to warm up. They operate from a routine and will resist sudden change. This can be an issue if married to an extrovert that can change immediately. Phlegmatics are loyal to their mate, family oriented, and like to stay at home. They make good companions because they are patient and tolerant of other people's shortcomings. They are slow to get upset and do not show much emotion. Their mate may not know that they are unhappy about something that happened years ago. Phlegmatics tend to be grudge holders. They are not flexible, spontaneous, impulsive, or talkative. This requires a lot of patience from their mate. They typically do not like to be on the go or be with people other than family. Phlegmatics are more of a spectator of life, rather than a participant. They dislike tension and conflict. Phlegmatics easily procrastinate. Their motto is, "why do today what can be put off until tomorrow."

These tendencies will be modified depending on the influence of the second temperament and their maturity level.

THE PHLEGMATIC | HIGH S BLENDS

THE INSPECTOR
PHLEGMATIC-CHOLERIC | S-D BLEND

The Phlegmatic-Choleric blend is driven by two temperament needs. The primary temperament need is to be accommodating. The secondary need is to get results. Either need may dominate their behavior depending on the situation.

When the Phlegmatic and the Choleric natural tendencies are combined in the Inspector's blend, it produces an accommodating, result-oriented person who is unyielding in their routine and very determined. The Inspector is one of the least frequently found patterns.

DESCRIPTION

Inspectors prefer to be with family or a few close friends most of the time. When focused on a goal they will pursue it with unbending determination. They have an anchored determination to follow their routine or complete a task.

They are accommodating, industrious, and independent (loners). The Inspector will have a firm, stoic expression (flat affect) and will rarely smile. They are calm, steady, and persevering. They can be very blunt, stubborn, and sarcastic. They rarely show emotion or affection.

Inspectors want to operate by themselves and set their own pace. Once their mind is made up they will resist any other method of approach. They seek challenging assignments without close supervision. Inspectors prefer work of a routine and technical nature rather than involvement with people.

This focused individual brings a deceptively intense approach to the task. Being low-key outwardly, their involvement in a task is not easily observed. They are successful because of their commitment to completing a task. After starting a project, they are tenacious and will fight for their objectives. Inspectors are very independent, questioning, and thorough in their approach and will follow through until the task is completed.

Inspectors become sleepy when sitting still after only a few minutes. They are very dependable, routine, and loyal (they change their routine slowly). Inspectors are dispassionate anchors of reality. They need time to warm-up before showing friendliness.

STRENGTHS

The Inspector is dependable, determined, and not easily distracted. They are accommodating to a point, as long as it does not interfere with their routine. Once they accept a task they are unyielding in their commitment to completing it, and they rarely give up. They are loyal to others. They exhibit calmness in a crisis.

WEAKNESSES

The Inspector's effectiveness in relationships and productivity in their career is often hindered because of their resistance to change and bluntness when communicating with others. They project aloofness. They are possessive to a fault and can be very stubborn if it is not their idea. They can be indecisive.

NEEDS

The Inspector will perform at their best and will be highly motivated if their natural, basic needs are met, such as: having a low-key environment, time to change their routine, and clear, specific instructions on when to start and stop a task. They need the opportunity to steadily work toward results. They are very independent and need the freedom to establish their own pace.

FEARS

Fear tends to create anger. Fear is a primary emotion and anger is a secondary emotion. The Inspector may respond with anger if any of their natural fears are realized, such as: too much social involvement with people, abstract ideas, sudden change, loss of independence, and interference with family time.

RESPONSE TO PRESSURE

When under pressure or stress, the Inspector will likely withdraw and worry.

They will become blunt and sarcastic. They may procrastinate and take no action. They often release their frustration with an outburst of anger and/or excessive sleeping.

CAUSES OF PROCRASTINATION

Inspectors will likely procrastinate because the activity does not fit their routine and they do not want to change--they are capable of strongly resisting change to their routine. Sometimes they procrastinate because they are not sure how to accommodate everyone involved and they are trying to avoid conflict.

Inspectors need slight but consistent pressure to encourage them to act, and sometimes a lot of pushing is needed. They need to see it is okay to act although not everyone will be accommodated. They also need to consider that a change in their routine is not always undesirable.

TRAITS NEEDED FOR BALANCE

In order to be a more balanced person, the Inspector needs to incorporate the following into their behavior: more social involvement, showing friendliness, being more sensitive to others, expressions of warm emotion, flexibility, and a willingness to consider change more quickly.

KEYS TO RELATING

To effectively relate to the Inspector show personal interest, be accepting, and practical. Be specific when explaining concepts. Be persistent, push gently, and use visual aids because they are concrete people. They need to see, touch, and feel what you are talking about. They do not visualize well.

In conversations, the Inspector responds best to words, such as: support, traditional, realistic, care, family, practical, and results. The Phlegmatic temperament in general likes to hear the words, "I sincerely appreciate...."

Be aware that they lack a sense-of-urgency and will resist and resent being pushed to complete a request. The more you push the more likely they will push back and entrench in their position.

Give them time to adjust to a change in their routine--especially sudden change which they do not handle very well. Be prepared for the Inspector to be stubborn, opinionated, and aloof. Inspectors can be coldly blunt and tactless with others. They may conceal their grievances and be a grudge-holder.

THE HARMONIZER
PHLEGMATIC-SANGUINE | S-I BLEND

The Phlegmatic-Sanguine blend is driven by two temperament needs. The primary temperament need is to be accommodating. The secondary need is to be accepted socially. Either need may dominate their behavior depending on the requirements of the situation.

When the Phlegmatic and the Sanguine natural tendencies are combined in the Harmonizer's blend, it produces an accommodating, people-oriented person who is routine, friendly, and tolerant of others. The Harmonizer is the most friendly of the all the Phlegmatic blends. The Harmonizer is a frequently found pattern.

DESCRIPTION

Harmonizers prefer a mostly private, routine existence, and involvement with family and a few friends. The Phlegmatic-Sanguine has a stoic expression but will, at times, show a natural smile. They are more friendly than the other Phlegmatic blends. They easily accept others. Harmonizers are accommodating and easy to be associated with both in the work environment and as a friend. They have difficulty confronting or pressuring people. They stubbornly resist change--especially sudden change.

They need some social involvement. Harmonizers are loyal, consistent, and dependable. They are naturally service minded. They will often work when they are ill. They are very independent minded and want to operate by themselves and set their own pace. They learn by doing (hands on). They need to be shown how to do a task, and then left alone. Once their mind is made up, they will resist any other method or approach.

Harmonizers can do routine work but will need some change during the day. They have a very difficult time saying no and will often take on more than they can do just to please others. Harmonizers are nice, likable people and have a very pleasant, soft voice. They are more friendly after warming-up and can be very talkative at times.

STRENGTHS

The Harmonizer is naturally accommodating, predictable, and patient. They have a gentle friendliness. They easily accept others and they are loyal to their family and friends. They are dependable and seek a routine for stability. They avoid conflict, although they can become assertive to restore harmony and peace to their environment.

WEAKNESSES

The Harmonizer's effectiveness in relationships and productivity in their career is often hindered because of their resistance to change, fear of confronting others and indecisiveness. They may try to accommodate or please everyone. They can be very stubborn when asked to suddenly change their routine. They are possessive of relationships and material things. They often lack a sense of urgency to get the task done. They may talk excessively at times.

NEEDS

The Harmonizer will perform at their best and will be highly motivated if their natural, basic needs are met, such as: being of service to others, having a routine schedule, and a specific, concrete plan to follow. They need detailed, specific instructions on when to start and stop a task. They need some social activity and play time.

FEARS

Fear tends to create anger. Fear is a primary emotion and anger is a secondary emotion. The Harmonizer may respond with anger if any of their natural fears are realized (or they perceive they may be), such as: disharmony, sudden change in their routine, needing to put pressure on or confront others, and infringement on their home life.

RESPONSE TO PRESSURE

When under pressure or stress, the Harmonizer will likely worry, procrastinate, talk excessively, withdraw and sleep excessively. They may give in outwardly when being pressured just to avoid the conflict, but inwardly they will be of the same opinion.

CAUSES OF PROCRASTINATION

Harmonizers will likely procrastinate because the activity does not fit their routine and they do not want to change. Sometimes they procrastinate because they are not sure how to accommodate everyone involved and they are trying to avoid conflict.

Harmonizers need slight but consistent pressure to encourage them to act. They need to see that it is okay to act, although not everyone will be accommodated.

TRAITS NEEDED FOR BALANCE

In order to be a more balanced person, the Harmonizer needs to incorporate the following into their behavior: willingness to accept change (especially when the change is sudden), directness, decisiveness, willingness to confront others, and to say no on occasion.

KEYS TO RELATING

To effectively relate to the Harmonizer, be low-key emotionally, be warm and practical, and show personal interest. Be specific when explaining concepts. Be persistent, push gently, and use visual aids because they are concrete people-- they need to see, touch, and feel what you are explaining.

In conversation, the Harmonizer responds well to words and phrases, such as: support, family, friend, practical, traditional, routine, stable, realistic, flexible, care, accommodate, relationship, and especially the phrase, "I sincerely appreciate...."

The Harmonizer does not respond well to pressure of any kind. They prefer low-key, gentle relationships. They lack a sense-of-urgency and will resist being pushed to accomplish a request. The more you push, the more they will push back. Give them time to adjust to a change in their routine--especially sudden change, which they do not handle very well.

If they become upset with someone they may conceal their grievances and be a grudge-holder. Be prepared to listen because the Harmonizer tends to talk excessively at times.

THE HELPER
PHLEGMATIC-MELANCHOLY | S-C BLEND

The Phlegmatic-Melancholy blend is driven by two temperament needs. The primary temperament need is to be accommodating. The secondary need is to do things right. Either need may dominate their behavior depending on the requirements of the situation.

When the Phlegmatic and the Melancholy natural tendencies are combined in the Helper blend, it produces an accommodating, routine person who is concerned about quality. The Helper is the most consistent of all the Phlegmatic blends. The Helper is a frequently found pattern and is at times referred to as The Supporter.

DESCRIPTION

Helpers need to be alone most of the time and spend time with their family at home. They are nice, gracious, and cordial people. They rarely show emotion or affection. They are routine, consistent, and loyal. They have a strong desire for independence and will resist change, especially sudden change. Helpers are accepting and tolerant of others. They have a stoic expression (flat affect). Helpers are more consistent than the other Phlegmatic blends.

They are naturally routine, accommodating, family-oriented, and passive about most things. They are patient, self-controlled, and deliberate in their actions. They are amiable and easygoing and slowly pace their way through life. They tend to have a long life-span because they do not get stressed out like the other temperament blends.

This determined and persistent person brings a deceptively intense approach to the task. Being low-keyed outwardly, their emotional involvement in a task is not easily observed. They are calm, steady, and persevering. Helpers are successful because of persistence. After starting a project, they will usually see it through to completion--they rarely give up.

Helpers are independent, questioning, and thorough in their approach, and will follow through. They want to operate by themselves and set their own pace. Helpers are very possessive of family time, material things, and friends. Once their mind is made up, they will resist any other method or approach.

Helpers prefer work of a technical nature and involvement with a limited number of people. Helpers approach a task with calculated moderation. They are always willing to help those they consider to be their friend. They have a difficult time saying no. They have great difficulty confronting or pressuring others, but when they do, they can be sarcastic and slightly offensive. They become sleepy when sitting still after only a few minutes.

STRENGTHS

The Helper is naturally accommodating and service-oriented which promotes their effectiveness in relationships, and productivity in their career. They are calm, patient, and loyal. They are accepting of others and possess a gentle, gracious, and genuine friendliness. They follow their routine strongly and are therefore predictable and dependable.

WEAKNESSES

The Helper's effectiveness in relationships and productivity in their career is often hindered because of their resistance to change, especially sudden change. They tend to be too accommodating because of their fear of conflict and tension. They recoil at the thought of confronting someone. They tend to worry excessively and they can be too possessive, stubborn, passive, and indecisive.

NEEDS

The Helper will perform at their best and will be highly motivated if their basic, natural needs are met such as: to be of service to others, having a routine, having clear, concrete instructions on when to start and stop a task. They need a low-key environment to have the freedom to be productive (at their own pace). They need to be shown how to do a task and then left alone.

FEARS

Fear tends to create anger. Fear is a primary emotion and anger is a secondary emotion. The Helper may respond with anger if any of their natural fears are realized, such as: change in their routine without prior conditioning, a need to put even slight pressure on people, infringement on home life, or disunity, especially within their family.

RESPONSE TO PRESSURE

When under pressure or stress, the Helper will likely worry excessively and then withdraw to sleep. The more intense the stress, the longer the Helper will sleep long hours. They may become critical and sarcastic.

CAUSES OF PROCRASTINATION

Helpers will likely procrastinate because the activity does not fit their routine and they do not want to change. Sometimes they procrastinate because they are not sure how to accommodate everyone involved and they are trying to avoid tension and conflict.

Helpers need slight but consistent pressure to encourage them to act. They need to see that it is okay to take action, although not everyone will be accommodated.

TRAITS NEEDED FOR BALANCE

In order to be a more balanced person, the Helper needs to incorporate the following into their behavior: willingness to accept change, assertiveness, willingness to confront, willingness to show more emotion and affection, willingness to be more decisive, and flexible.

KEYS TO RELATING

To effectively relate to the Helper, show personal interest and remove the risk of tension or conflict. Do not show too much emotion. Be warm, personable, and practical. Be specific when explaining concepts. Give them a hands-on opportunity--they are concrete people and need visual aids.

In conversation, the Helper responds best to words and phrases, such as: support, family, practical, friend, routine, stable, traditional, realistic, care, relationship, and especially the phrase, "I sincerely appreciate...."

CHAPTER **NINE**

THE MELANCHOLY | HIGH C
PRIMARY & TEMPERAMENT BLENDS

Melancholies are detailed-oriented and operate from a plan. They are very private. They influence their environment by adhering to the existing rules and by doing things right. They have a cautious, tentative response designed to reduce tension in an unfavorable environment. After developing a plan, the Melancholy can become aggressive to restore peace in an unfavorable situation. The Melancholy temperament has three combinations and four common patterns:

COMBINATION	PATTERN
Melancholy-Choleric	Trainer-Idealist
Melancholy-Sanguine	Diplomat
Melancholy-Phlegmatic	Analyst

The traits of the primary temperament, Melancholy, will be altered or modified in some significant way due to the influence of the secondary temperament. Remember, there are at least three levels of intensity of a temperament: classic, moderate, and mild. Some Melancholies will be very strong, others somewhat strong, and still others more mild.

Melancholies are introverted, logical, analytical, and factual in communication. They need information, time alone to think, and a detailed plan in order to function effectively without anxiety.

Melancholies respond to others in a slow, cautious, and indirect manner. They are reserved and suspicious until they are sure of your intentions. Melancholies probe for the hidden meaning behind your words. They are timid, may appear unsure, and have a serious expression. Melancholies are self-sacrificing, gifted, and they can be a perfectionist.

Melancholies are conscientious, picky, and can be sensitive to what others think of their work. They have anxiety about the present and future. They tend to have guilt feelings but fail to realize that guilt will not change the past nor will worry change the future. They allow guilt and worry to rob them of enjoying now.

Melancholies are well organized. However, on occasion, they may keep things cluttered, but they will know what is in the piles. They are determined to make the right and best decision so they will collect lots of information and ask very specific questions, and sometimes they will ask the same question several times. They may take excessive time to think through their options before making a decision. Even then, they may not be sure it is the right, and best decision.

Melancholies need reassurance, feedback, and reasons why they should do something. They can be moody, which is usually related to their negative evaluation of people or events.

Melancholies fear taking risks, making wrong decisions, and being viewed as incompetent. They tend to have a negative attitude toward something new until they have had time to think it through. Melancholies are skeptical about almost everything, but they are creative and capable people. They tend to get bored with something once they get it figured out.

The theologian Ole Hallesby (1962) in *Temperament and the Christian Fatih* says this about the Melancholy:

> In this temperament, it is feeling which predominates. Fewer impressions are allowed to enter, but these few are carefully considered and analyzed thoroughly.

The following represents Melancholies in general but individual differences will occur. What a person is exposed to from an early age plays a vital role in these areas but remember an individual is still responsible for the choices they make. Regardless of one's natural tendencies, discipline applied in any area will control and overcome weaknesses or extreme behavior. The goal is to become a well-balanced person, being in control of thoughts, feelings, and behavior.

MONEY MANAGEMENT

Melancholies view money as a safety net because they tend to worry excessively about the future. Their natural tendency is to be cautious and careful about spending. They will, however, spend money on a high quality item and the latest gadget. Melancholies are guided by logic over emotion when saving or investing money. They often say that they, "do not like to waste money," but they fail to realize that is a relative statement. What is waste to one may not be to another.

TIME MANAGEMENT

Melancholies tend to be a good manager of time. They are usually very conscientious about being where they are supposed to be on time. Melancholies will use part of their daily, alone time to process information and to develop their plan. They enjoy staying up late at night to work because they feel safe and free from interruptions. Melancholies get more accomplished when alone. Their stress level increases when pressured to meet a time line.

DECISION MAKING

Melancholies take an excessive amount of time to make a decision. They are paralyzed by their need to analyze all the information (several times) to arrive at the right and best decision. It's the paralysis of analysis syndrome. They will ask many questions in order to collect enough information that will be analyzed twice! Melancholies often get stuck because they tend to think too much about the wrong thing!

RELATIONSHIPS

Melancholies build relationships slowly and carefully, and will have only a few close friends. They will be very guarded about personal information until they are comfortable with the person. Melancholies will warm up quickly if they feel accepted. Once comfortable they will be the affectionate, warm, cozy, "sit by the fire" type.

LEADERSHIP STYLE

Melancholies manage with controlled emotions and strict guidelines. They will be logical and thoughtful, adhering to the established rules and regulations of their environment. Productivity is often hindered because of the amount of time taken to make a decision. Melancholies try to determine the right and best thing to do. They usually take a team approach to management, wanting everyone to cooperate. Melancholies will have an increased level of anxiety when they need to confront someone.

FOOD

Melancholies view food as fuel. This group will analyze what is in the food they consume. They will research what is better or best to put in their body. Melancholies exercise the most restraint when eating and usually stay relatively slim. Overall, Melancholies exercise the most self-control.

AS A MATE

Melancholies can be very affectionate once they feel safe and secure. They are considerate about little things and will remember birthdays and anniversaries.

Before making a decision, Melancholies will need lots of information. They must also have a plan from which to operate and that can be an issue if they marry an extrovert, who is impulsive. A deviation in their plan, without a reason, will almost always be met with strong resistance.

Melancholies are not social by nature and will have to be pushed to be with people other than family. Once at a social event, they may want to leave soon after they arrive (unless it is family). They can be critical and demeaning in their evaluation of people and events and if married to an optimistic mate this will cause conflict. Melancholies like to be in control because they think their way is the best--this is because they have spent hours thinking about everything!

Melancholies are logical, moody and need time alone to think. Without alone time, they will not function effectively. They also need feedback and reassurance in order to function without anxiety. Getting this from their mate will help facilitate a healthy relationship. Be aware that when you argue with a Melancholy they may get historical. They may bring up everything you've ever done wrong, with dates!

These tendencies will be modified depending on the influence of the second temperament and their maturity level.

THE TRAINER
MELANCHOLY-CHOLERIC | C-D BLEND

The Melancholy-Choleric blend is driven by two temperament needs. The primary temperament need is to do things right. The secondary need is to get results. The Trainer, therefore, will influence their environment by striving to do things right while overcoming opposition to get results. Either need may dominate behavior depending on the situation.

When the Melancholy and the Choleric natural tendencies are combined in the Trainer's blend, it produces a detail-oriented person who pushes to get results. Trainers are systematic, precise thinkers, and they follow self-imposed, strict procedures in both their business and personal lives. Trainers have firm, serious expressions, and they rarely smile. The Trainer is a somewhat common pattern.

DESCRIPTION

Trainers are more forceful, pushy, and blunt than the other Melancholy blends. They have a strong drive to teach others what they know. They can be abrasive and offensive when communicating with others. The Trainer is a systematic, precise thinker who follows procedures in both their business and personal lives. Trainers are attentive to details and push to have things done correctly according to their predetermined standards. They have high standards for themselves and others. They can be a perfectionist about many things. They will resist change until the reasons are explained, defended, and accepted.

They are sensitive and conscientious. They can behave in a diplomatic manner, except when it comes to deviating from standards they have accepted. Trainers can be too forceful in insisting the right way (or their way) be followed.

They are not socially active, preferring work and privacy to being with people. Trainers tend to have difficulty in relationships because they are not flexible and they can be brief and abrasive when communicating with others.

Trainers tend to make decisions slowly because of their need to collect and analyze information (several times) until they are sure of the right and best course of action.

STRENGTHS

The Trainer is naturally analytical and result-oriented. They are creative problem solvers with high standards. They like to do things right. They have a strong sense of justice (right vs. wrong). They are organized and will operate from a well thought through plan. Once they commit to a goal, they usually follow it to completion.

WEAKNESSES

The Trainer's effectiveness in relationships and productivity in their career is often hindered because of their unrealistic expectations, their high standards, and critical attitude. They can be blunt and sarcastic and even condescending when frustrated. They can be abrasive in conversation.

They can be indecisive until they collect sufficient information to make the best decision. The Trainer can be moody which is typically caused by a tendency to think too much about the wrong thing.

NEEDS

The Trainer will perform at their best and will be highly motivated if their natural, basic needs are met, such as: having a structured environment with clear, concrete rules and procedures to follow; having a task that requires working with detail and analysis; having time to collect information, having time alone to think, having time to organize, and having time to develop a plan.

The Trainer needs a reason why something should be done and will be paralyzed until the task becomes logical to them. They then need feedback and reassurance as they are involved in completing the task to be sure they are proceeding correctly.

FEARS

Fear tends to create anger. Fear is a primary emotion and anger is a secondary emotion. The Trainer may respond with anger if any of their natural fears are realized, such as: not having a detailed plan to follow, being wrong, losing emotional control, being disorganized, not having privacy, having conflict, and having too much social involvement with those outside their family or close circle of friends.

RESPONSE TO PRESSURE

When under pressure or stress, the Trainer will likely become negative and suspicious. They will release their frustration by withdrawing or by having an outburst of anger. When the Trainer withdraws, they are thinking, reviewing, and trying to solve the problem and develop a plan. When frustrated, they often want to quit whatever they are involved in doing.

They struggle with guilt feelings and can be apologetic. They have difficulty going to sleep because they are analyzing something, anything, everything (again and again).

CAUSES OF PROCRASTINATION

Trainers will likely procrastinate because they are not sure of the right or best thing to do. They usually take lots of time to think through their options.

Frustration (and procrastination) occurs when the secondary need for results interferes with the primary need to think and plan. They need others that they respect to be objective and help them decide on the best approach.

TRAITS NEEDED FOR BALANCE

In order to be a more balanced person, the Trainer needs to incorporate the following into their behavior: expressing opinions without negative emotion, a positive outlook, positive self-talk, and more friendliness. The Trainer also needs to become more socially involved.

KEYS TO RELATING

To effectively relate to the Trainer, be specific and factual, stress quality, and understand their need for a plan. Show concern and tolerate their abruptness.

In conversation, the Trainer responds best to words such as: logical, facts, precise, practical, quality, detail, efficient, and results.

Be careful, the Trainer can take personal criticism better than criticism of their work. The reason is that they have put so much thought into their work and they are sure it is correct. If you have a logical and/or factual reason why something isn't correct or will not work, they will listen.

THE IDEALIST
MELANCHOLY-PHLEGMATIC-CHOLERIC |
C-S-D BLEND

The Melancholy-Phlegmatic-Choleric blend is driven by several temperament needs. The primary temperament need is to do things right. The secondary need is to be accommodating. A third temperament need is to get results.

When the Melancholy, Phlegmatic, and Choleric temperaments are combined in the Idealist's blend, it produces a very detail-oriented person who tries to be accommodating while pushing for results and striving to be perfect in all that they do. These three temperament needs are often in conflict with each other, causing anxiety and stress. This blend is a classic perfectionist.

Idealists are unique because of the influence of the Choleric temperament. It is the influence of this third temperament that causes the Idealist to push their ideal standards to perfection. The Idealist is a somewhat common pattern.

DESCRIPTION

Idealists need information, time alone to think and to develop a plan to guide them in everything they do. They are systematic and precise thinkers. They have high, sometimes unrealistic standards, for themselves and others. They are very attentive to details and push to have things done correctly, according to the standards they have accepted.

Idealists are conscientious in work, requiring accuracy and high standards. They have feelings of guilt and tend to be apologetic about things that are not their fault. They may appear detached or aloof on occasions--this is because they are in deep thought. Idealists normally behave in a diplomatic manner but may become blunt and make condescending remarks if their standards have been violated. Idealists may then become forceful, insisting the right way be followed.

They are not interested in social events, preferring privacy, family, and a few close friends. Idealists make decisions slowly because of their need to collect and analyze information until they are sure of the best and right course of action. They resist change until reasons are explained, defended, and accepted. They have difficulty going to sleep because they are analyzing what happened yesterday, or today, or what will happen tomorrow, or next week. They are also planning their activities for the next day.

STRENGTHS

The Idealist is a natural perfectionist. They are logical, analytical, tenacious, and strive to do everything exactly right. They push to maintain very high standards in everything they do. They like to follow predetermined procedures so they will not make a mistake. They are organized and usually neat. They have a strong sense of justice and will fight for a cause.

WEAKNESSES

The Idealist's effectiveness in relationships and productivity in their career is often hindered because of their high standards and unrealistic expectations. They are inflexible and resist change until they've had time to think about it several times. They tend to be critical of others, moody, and indecisive.

They are easily frustrated and exhibit a demeaning attitude and may withdraw when things do not go their way. They rehearse negative self-talk that keeps them from enjoying the moment--they worry about what should have been, what could have been, and what ought to have been. They seem never satisfied with who they are or where they are in life. They continue to seek perfection but never seem to achieve the ideal they so strongly desire. It's like a donkey walking toward the carrot that is dangling at the end of a stick. The stick is tied to their back and hanging over their head--the donkey moves and the carrot moves. Perfection will be achieved only when the donkey gets the carrot! Since you cannot live perfectly in an imperfect world, do your best and that will always be enough.

NEEDS

The Idealist will perform at their best and will be highly motivated if their natural, basic needs are met, such as: being able to collect information, having time alone to analyze and plan, having concrete, clear rules and procedures, and having a detailed plan to follow. The Idealist needs a structured environment and procedures to follow or they cannot function effectively. Without these needs being met the Idealist will experience a high degree of anxiety.

FEARS

Fear tends to create anger. Fear is a primary emotion and anger is a secondary emotion. The Idealist may respond with anger if any of their natural fears are realized (or they perceive they may be realized), such as: not having enough information, not having a plan, losing emotional control, being wrong, not having privacy, being disorganized, being ridiculed, having conflict, and having too much social involvement with those outside their family or close circle of friends.

RESPONSE TO PRESSURE

When under pressure or stress, the Idealist will likely become negative, suspicious, and may want to quit a project or leave a relationship. They release frustration by withdrawing to think, review and plan, or they have an outburst of anger. Such a display is usually followed by deep regret and an apology.

CAUSES OF PROCRASTINATION

Idealists will likely procrastinate because they are not sure of the right or best thing to do. They usually take lots of time to think through their options. Frustration occurs (therefore procrastination) when the need to think and plan conflicts with the need to accommodate others, and get results. They need others to be objective to get them through the details, and help them decide on the best, most practical approach.

TRAITS NEEDED FOR BALANCE

In order to be a more balanced person, the Idealist needs to incorporate the following into their behavior: expressing opinions without being critical, having more realistic standards and expectations, showing more flexibility, showing more friendliness, and having more social involvement.

KEYS TO RELATING

To effectively relate to the Idealist, be very specific and factual. Stress logic and quality. Show concern about their concerns. Be willing to answer their detailed questions several times.

In conversation, the Idealist responds best to words such as: logical, facts, precise, plan, right, best, practical, quality, detail, and efficient.

THE DIPLOMAT
MELANCHOLY-SANGUINE | C-I BLEND

The Melancholy-Sanguine blend is driven by two temperament needs. The primary temperament need is to do things right. The secondary need is to be accepted socially. Either need may dominate their behavior depending on the requirements of the situation.

When the Melancholy and the Sanguine natural tendencies are combined in the Diplomat's blend, it produces a detail-oriented person who, enjoys some social activity. The Diplomat is the most friendly of all the Melancholy blends. The Diplomat is a frequently found pattern.

DESCRIPTION

Diplomats need to be alone most of time and they need to be with people some of the time. When alone they will likely review the day and plan tomorrow. Diplomats are more friendly than the other Melancholy blends and they have a natural smile. They are analytical, systematic, and sensitive to the needs of others. This is a versatile, productive individual who works well with most everyone. Diplomats like to have fun and laugh when they feel comfortable and accepted. They can be very talkative at times. They have high personal ambitions but often fail to achieve their dreams because of their fear of failure.

Diplomats tend to be well-balanced and they are precise thinkers who tend to follow procedures in both their business and personal lives. They are mostly well organized. Diplomats are attentive to detail and can be openly friendly at times. Diplomats will be more friendly toward new people after they warm up. They like to do things correctly according to their standards. They like quality and status things. They are very conscientious. Diplomats need some mobility rather than sitting for long periods of time. They can be very sensitive to criticism and react with strong emotion.

Diplomats make decisions slowly because they are analyzing their options. They need to be sure of the right and best course of action. This is especially true when involved in a new project.

At times they may have difficulty going to sleep due to excessive worry. They generally like to ease into the day instead of rushing into activity. They prefer others to wait awhile before talking to them after they awaken.

The Diplomat struggles with having guilt feelings, even about something that is not their fault. They tend to be apologetic.

STRENGTHS

The Diplomat is naturally private, analytical, and they enjoy being socially active some of the time. Most of their social activity will be with family and friends rather than with new people and/or groups. They are gentle and diplomatic when dealing with people. They are conscientious, thoughtful, and good at solving people problems. They have a desire for quality in whatever they do and they are creative. They can make an impressive detailed presentation to a group. They make excellent teachers.

WEAKNESSES

The Diplomat's effectiveness in relationships and productivity in their career is often hindered because of their indecisiveness, sensitivity, unrealistic expectations, and high standards. They can be moody and inflexible. They can also be critical of others and, at times, they talk too much. They tend to withdraw under pressure and will avoid confronting others.

NEEDS

The Diplomat will be motivated to perform at their best if their natural, basic needs are met, such as: a structured environment with clear rules and procedures to follow with some social contact with people, and some flexibility in their schedule. They become restless if they have to sit for long periods of time to do a task. They need time alone to think, analyze, and to develop a plan.

FEARS

Fear tends to create anger. Fear is a primary emotion and anger is a secondary emotion. The Diplomat may respond with anger if any of their natural fears are realized (or they perceive they may be realized), such as: not having a plan, being around tension or conflict, being wrong, losing emotional control, losing social acceptance, being embarrassed, not having privacy or alone time, or being ridiculed.

They also have a fear of confronting or pressuring others.

RESPONSE TO PRESSURE

When under pressure or stress, the Diplomat will likely become negative, suspicious, will likely demonstrate strong emotion, and may want to quit. They release frustration by withdrawing to think, review, and plan, or by talking excessively with intense emotion.

CAUSES OF PROCRASTINATION

Diplomats will likely procrastinate because they are not sure of the right or best way to do a task. They usually take lots of time to think through their options.

Frustration occurs (therefore procrastination) when the secondary need for contact with people interferes with the primary need to be alone to think. Diplomats need others to be objective and help them decide on their options and best approach.

TRAITS NEEDED FOR BALANCE

In order to be a more balanced person, the Diplomat needs to incorporate the following into their behavior: developing realistic standards, learning to be assertive, taking action to achieve goals, and expressing opinions without being emotional--they need to learn to be matter-of-fact in communication.

KEYS TO RELATING

To effectively relate to the Diplomat be friendly, factual, smile, and be lighthearted. Be logical, specific, and stress quality. Remove the risk of making a bad decision or being embarrassed.

In conversation, the Diplomat responds best to words such as: logical, facts, precise, practical, quality, detail, efficient, together, fun, and exciting.

Diplomats tend to bog down in details especially when decisions need to be made. They may become overly dependent on others looking for someone to make the decision for them. They hesitate to act without precedent. They may yield their position to avoid conflict or controversy, but still be anchored in their opinion. Diplomats tend to become defensive when criticized, threatened, or pushed to complete a task. Remember, Diplomats can be very sensitive to what others think.

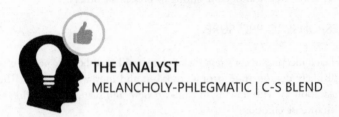

THE ANALYST
MELANCHOLY-PHLEGMATIC | C-S BLEND

The Melancholy-Phlegmatic blend is driven by two temperament needs. The primary temperament need is to do things right. The secondary need is to be accommodating. Either need may dominate their behavior depending on the requirements of the situation. When the Melancholy and the Phlegmatic natural tendencies are combined in the Analyst's blend, it produces a detail-oriented person who is accommodating and will cautiously plan their way through life. The Analyst is the most consistent of all the Melancholy blends. The Analyst is a frequently found pattern.

DESCRIPTION

Analysts prefer being alone most of the time. They are not socially active, preferring to be with family or a few close friends. When at a social event they usually do not stay for a long period of time. In order to function well, they need information, time alone to think, and a plan from which to operate. They like working privately on a project. They are usually very well organized and tend to operate from a list--it may be written down or just in their head. If they are not neatly organized, they know what's in those piles!

Analysts are pleasant and accommodating people who tend to seek a structured environment requiring attention to detail. They have a self-sacrificing, self-critical nature and struggle with guilt feelings about things that are not their fault. Analysts are more conscientious and private than the other Melancholy blends. They are systematic, precise thinkers who tend to follow procedures in both their business and personal lives. They will withdraw from aggressive people. They will have difficulty putting pressure on others. The Analyst will become aggressive to restore harmony to their environment.

Analysts make decisions slowly because of their need to collect and review information until they are sure of the right and best course of action. This is especially true when involved in a new project. They will be a bit of a perfectionist at times but not like the Idealist pattern.

Analysts are good at anticipating problems and figuring out solutions, but not good at taking action. Analysts have difficulty going to sleep because they are thinking.

Analysts feel safe to think, review, and plan when they stay up after the rest of the family has gone to bed. Males in particular like staying up late at night to flip through the TV channels. Someone said that men do not want to watch TV, they just want to see what's on the next channel!

They have a strong sense of justice. They like quality things. They resist change until reasons are explained, defended, and accepted. They resist changing their plan, especially if the change is sudden. They need pushing to be sociable beyond their family and close friends. The Analyst often has a Sanguine as a close friend because they like their fun nature and carefree attitude.

STRENGTHS

The Analyst has a natural drive to analyze everything and operate from a detailed plan and list. They like to do things right according to predetermined rules and procedures. They are well organized and give attention to detail. They are usually diplomatic when dealing with others. They are quietly creative and good at solving technical problems. They work well alone. If they have respect for those with whom they are associated, they will cooperate and be a good, helpful team member.

WEAKNESSES

The Analyst's effectiveness in relationships and productivity in their career is often hindered because of their negative self-talk, critical attitude, and being too sensitive. They often fail to take action on their detailed plan because they are never sure if they have all the necessary information. They often have unrealistic expectations for themselves and others. They can be moody and will withdraw to be alone to think. They often bring misery upon themselves because of being too picky and having a negative view of people, events, and life in general.

NEEDS

The Analyst will perform at their best and will be highly motivated if their natural, basic needs are met, such as: having a structured environment with clear rules and procedures to follow, having time to organize, having time to gather information, and having time to think and develop a plan. They need detailed work and privacy. They need feedback and reassurance that what they are doing is appropriate and acceptable. Once they accept the feedback and reassurance they have received, they are able to continue and move forward with efficiency.

FEARS

Fear tends to create anger. Fear is a primary emotion and anger is a secondary emotion. Analysts may respond with anger if any of their natural fears are realized (or they perceive they may be realized), such as: criticism of their work, being wrong, conflict, loss of emotional control, being disorganized, and not having a plan.

RESPONSE TO PRESSURE

When under pressure or stress, the Analyst will likely become negative, critical, and suspicious, and want to quit what they are doing. If the Analyst actually does quit they usually change their mind after a short while.

The Analyst releases frustration by withdrawing to worry and to develop a plan. The greater the stress, the more alone time is needed to process through the issues. During a time of excessive worry, the Analyst will sleep less. On occasion, the Analyst may show intense emotion under pressure or stress which is usually followed by remorse, guilt feelings, and being apologetic.

CAUSES OF PROCRASTINATION

Analysts will likely procrastinate because they are not sure of the right or best thing to do. They usually take lots of time to think through their options before making a decision.

Analysts need others to be objective with them and help them decide on the best approach. They will need encouragement and slight pressure to help them take action.

TRAITS NEEDED FOR BALANCE

In order to be a more balanced person, the Analyst needs to incorporate the following into their behavior: follow-through with their plans and to express opinions without emotion by being matter-of-fact in their responses. They need more social involvement and to show more friendliness. The Analyst needs to develop a more positive outlook about life. The Analyst needs to develop the ability to make small-talk with others.

KEYS TO RELATING

To effectively relate to the Analyst, be low-key, specific, and factual. Avoid conflict and tension. Show concern about what concerns them. Be willing to answer their many, detailed questions. Remove the risk of making a bad decision by giving feedback and reassurance. Stress quality.

In conversation, the Analyst responds best to words such as: logical, plan, precise, practical, quality, details, and efficient.

When presenting the Analyst with a new idea it is best to allow them time to think about it before asking for a decision. It's effective to say, "let me give you something to think about."

CHAPTER **TEN**

CONCLUSION

The temperament model of behavior offers insightful information that will explain, basically and in part, why people do what they do. There are, of course, many factors that influence a person's behavior, as has been discussed. However, regardless of these factors, people will behave instinctively and consistently according to their temperament blend apart from the momentary experience of a strong expression of emotion.

This information enables you to gain a better understanding of why you do what you do and it gives you insight into your natural drives and needs. Once you understand your temperament blend, choose to use your natural strengths and overcome your natural weaknesses.

This information may also be applied to your relationships. By identifying the temperament blend of a person with whom you are associated (mate, children, family, friends, fellow workers, etc.), you are better able to understand their needs and you can have more effective communication. Decide to accept, tolerate, and appreciate the temperament differences you see in others. Adjust your natural tendencies to meet the temperament needs of others.

It is not appropriate to use this information to excuse selfish and immature behavior. Your temperament blend has natural needs, strengths, and weaknesses. Remember, it is your responsibility to use your natural strengths to be as productive as you can be and to overcome your natural weaknesses so you can be a more well-balanced person.

Dr. Henry Brandt said, "A mature man is one who is sufficiently objective about himself to know both his strengths and weaknesses and to create a planned program for overcoming his weaknesses."

What's your plan?

SPEAK MY LANGUAGE AND
I WILL LISTEN TO YOU.

ABOUT THE AUTHOR

John T. Cocoris has devoted his life since the early 1970's to develop the temperament model of behavior. John has a B.A. from Tennessee Temple University, a Masters of Theology (Th.M.) from Dallas Theological Seminary, a Masters in Counseling (M.A.) degree from Amberton University, a Doctorate in Psychology (Psy.D.) degree from California Coast University. John is a licensed counselor in the state of Texas.

John established Profile Dynamics in the early 1980's to develop and promote the temperament model of behavior for use in business and counseling. He has been a management consultant since 1984 and has worked with a variety of companies giving seminars for training managers and sales people. John has been interviewed on the radio and has been featured numerous times on COPE, a national cable TV talk show.

John has written many books and manuals about the temperament model including: *The Temperament Model of Behavior: Understanding Your Natural Tendencies; Born With A Creative Temperament, The Sanguine-Melancholy (I/C); The Problem Person In Your Life, Understanding People of Extremes; 7 Steps To A Better You: How To Develop Your Natural Tendencies; How To Discover and Develop Your Child's Temperament; Proverbs 22:6; 3 Reasons Why Christians Go to Counseling; A Therapist's Guide to The Temperament Model of Behavior; How to Supervise Others Using The Temperament Model of Behavior; Effective Selling Using The Temperament Model of Behavior; The DISC II Temperament Assessment; The DISC II Temperament Assessment User Guide; DISC II Library, 15 Pattern Series; The DISC 3 Temperament Assessment; The DISC 3 Temperament Assessment User Guide.*

To learn more about DISC and access all the resources mentioned above, visit:
http://fourtemperaments.com/

APPENDIX

JOHARI'S WINDOW

The Johari Window, named after the first names of its inventors, Joseph Luft and Harry Ingham, is one of the most useful models describing the process of human interaction. A four paned "window," as illustrated in the following page, divides personal awareness into four different categories, as represented by its four quadrants: open, blind, hidden, and unknown. The lines dividing the four panes are like window shades, which can move as an interaction progresses or more awareness is achieved.

1. The **OPEN** quadrant represents things that both
   I know about myself, and that you know about me.

2. The **BLIND** quadrant represents things that you
   know about me, but that I am unaware of.

3. The **HIDDEN** quadrant represents things that
   I know about myself, that you do not know.

4. The **UNKNOWN** quadrant represents things that neither
   I know about myself, nor you know about me.

Known to Self **OPEN** Known to Others	Unknown to Self **BLIND** Known to Others
Known to Self **HIDDEN** Unknown to Others	Unknown to Self **UNKNOWN** Unknown to others

REFERENCES

Allport, G.W. (1937). *Personality: A psychological interpretation.* New York, NY: Henry Holt & Company.

Arno, R.G., & Phyllis J. A. (2008). *The missing link: Revealing spiritual genetics.* Sarasota, FL: Peppertree Press.

Asher, J. (1987). Born to be shy. *Psychology Today, 21*(4), 56.

Buss, A. H., & Robert P. (1975). *A temperament theory of personality development.* New York, NY: John Wiley & Sons.

Chess, S., & Alexander, T. (1987). *Know your child.* New York, NY: BasicBooks, Inc., Publishers, 1987.

Dobson, J. C. (1987). *Parenting isn't for cowards: Dealing confidently with the frustrations of child-rearing.* Waco, TX: Word Books.

Eysenck, H. J. (1967). *The biological basis of personality.* Springfield, IL: Bannerstone House.

Eysenck, H. J. (1953). *The structure of human personality.* London: Methuen & Co. LTD.

Eysenck, H. J., & Eysenck, S. B. G. (1969). *Personality structure and measurement.* San Diego, CA: Robert R. Knapp, Publisher.

Eysenck, H. J., & Eysenck, M. W. (1985). *Personality and individual differences.* New York, NY : Plenum Press.

Frankl, V. (1946/2006). *Man's search for meaning.* (I. Lasch, Trans.). Boston, MA: Beacon Press.

Galen. (1968). *Galen's system of physiology and medicine.* (R.E. Siegel, Trans.). New York, NY: S. Karger.

Gier, J., & Downey, D. E. (1983). *Library of classical patterns.* Preformax Systems International, USA.

Glasser, W. (1999). *Choice theory: A new psychology of personal freedom.* New York, NY: Harper Perennial.

Hallesby, O. *Temperament & the christian faith.* (1962). Minneapolis, MN: Augsburg Publishing House.

Hippocrates. (1937). T*he genuine works of Hippocrates.* (F, Adams, Trans.). Baltimore, MD: The Williams & Wilkins Company. (Original work published 1939).

Kant, I. (1974). *Anthropology from a pragmatic point of view.* (M. J. Gregor, Trans.). The Hague, Netherlands: Martinus Nijhoff. (Original work published 1798).

Keirsey, D., & Bates, M. (1984). *Please understand me: Character & temperament types.* Del Mar, CA: Prometeus Nemesis Book Company.

Marston, W. M. (1979). *Emotions of normal people.* Minneapolis, MN: Persona Press, Inc.

Merrill, D. W., & Reid, R.H. (1981) *Personal styles & effective performance.* Bradner, PA: Chilton Book Company.

LaHaye, T. F. (1967). *Spirit controlled temperament.* Whaton: Tyndale House Publishers.

LaHaye, T. F. (1977). *Understanding the male temperament.* Old Tappan, NJ: Fleming H. Revell Co.

LaHaye, T. F. (1984). *Your temperament: Discover its potential.* Wheaton, IL: Tyndale House Publishers.

LaHaye, T. F. (1971). Transformed temperaments. Wheaton, IL: Tyndale House Publishers.

Littauer, F. (1992). *Personality plus.* Grand Rapids, MI: Fleming H. Revell.